I HATE CHILDREN AND OTHER HUMANIST STORIES

I HATE CHILDREN AND OTHER HUMANIST STORIES

Marv Friedlander

ISBN: 1981674381
ISBN 13: 9781981674381
Library of Congress Control Number: 2017919222
CreateSpace Independent Publishing Platform
North Charleston, South Carolina

Table of Contents

Being a humanist means trying to behave decently without expectation of rewards or punishment after you are dead. - Kurt Vonnegut Jr.

Most of us must learn to love people and use things rather than loving things and using people. - Roy T. Bennett

Snoopy: My dad used to run with the hounds, but his sympathies were elsewhere. He used to run on ahead and warn the rabbits! - Charles M. Schulz

Introduction

Strong as an eagle / brave as a vulture / go, go, go for Ethical Culture. I heard this cheer as a teenager when I attended a humanist-based religious organization. I figured it was a funny way to resolve a difficult rhyme scheme without taking ourselves too seriously.

Humanism at its best adheres to positive values, such as love of fairness, honesty, beauty, authenticity, boldness, trustworthiness, and wisdom. Conversely, humanism rejects adherence to negative values, such as greed, cynicism, rigidity, and dishonesty that lead to feelings of anger, intolerance, and entitlement.

What we value, what we hold up as a virtue, dictates how we act. For example, if we believe that honesty is best, we are more likely to forego stealing, cheating, and lying.

While believers seek moral direction through developing a personal relationship with God, humanists find meaning by seeking right relationships and right decisions based on reason and empathy. Some humanists accept the idea of a higher power; however, we are not dependent on a supreme being for our ethics. We act ethically by believing in the inherent worthiness of every person. We demonstrate this belief by attempting to bring out the best in others and, thereby, the best in ourselves. In this, humanism offers an optimistic view about the power of constructive relationships.

At first, I thought I was writing stories for a young audience. On further consideration, this book is appropriate for anyone who would like to explore humanist ideals delivered with a light touch.

I hope you enjoy,

Marv

Book 1

I Hate Children

We grown-ups pretend to like children. Some of us don't care a whit (a little bit) about them. We live with them. Heck, they are all around us. Perhaps I need a sign firmly planted in my front yard.

Kids: The farther away, the better the day.

At least that is how this curmudgeon (bad-tempered person) felt before meeting the little girl.

Oh yes, I am allowing her to help tell this story.

Time to begin.

I HATE CHILDREN.

They are too nosy and blunt; too needy and messy. They might present themselves nicely enough.

"Hi, Mister Griffith."

Then, they let you have it.

"Why are your legs so skinny?"

"Where's the rest of your hair?"

"Is that coffee breath?"

Children are fine when playing with their friends or minding their parents. It's after they get up close without any restraints (limits) that their irritating behavior begins. Kind of like a mosquito that suddenly whines right next to your ear. You want to automatically slap it away.

That was why I was chagrined (annoyed) when the guy next door, a guy even older than me, sold his house to a family. I figured it was bad luck all the way around.

Early in our marriage, I explained my views about children to my spouse (the person to whom someone is married).

"I would gladly have a child if we could adopt at a civilized age."

"Like when?" Virginia asked.

"Like when they become twenty-one," I replied.

I walked outside simply to gather the newspaper.

That's when I got my first glimpse of the little girl standing on her stoop smiling inanely (ridiculously) at me and blithely (carelessly) picking at her nose. This confirmed my worst fears. Pausing sufficiently between the words for sardonic effect (humor that makes fun of something or someone), I silently said, "nice, kid."

I HATE THAT OLD GRUMP.

I tried to smile at the elderly guy to show that I was a friendly person. No dice. He just frowned and then pretended that I wasn't there. We are neighbors. He ought to get to know me. I'm pleasant and friendly and small. How can I bother him?

When he sneered (made a nasty look) in my direction, I figured we might have a problem.

I TRIED TO IGNORE HER.

When I saw that brat looking my way, I offered her my best phony smile. The half-smile where I barely raise my top lip and slightly crinkle my eyes.

When an adult becomes tiresome (boring), you simply walk away with a cheery, 'See 'ya later.' Not so easy with kids. You try walking away and they are likely to follow you with a riot of requests.

"Can I get a drink, please, please? I'm thirsty."

"Do you have anything to eat? I like raisin bread."

And, the worst.

"Do you want to play catch?"

Why would I want to play catch with a smelly little person who is likely to fall and start bawling? Have I ever befriended you? Have I ever offered you the slightest encouragement? The little monsters are oblivious (not aware). They are bothersome. Even their parents want away time.

I MIGHT SEE IF HE NEEDS HELP.

I noticed that he was stiffly bending to pull some weeds from his lawn. I am lots closer to the ground. It's easy for me to bend over. Perhaps I'll just start grabbing weeds, so he gets the idea I want to help. Then, he might be a little friendlier. I got nothing else happening.

"What the heck are you doing?" he yelled.

"My name is Bailey. I live next door. I'm six. I was just trying to help," I replied in my friendliest voice.

"My name is Mr. Griffith. And, I don't want your help. Buzz off, girly," he growled.

"You are a mean sourpuss, butthead," I suggested.

"WHERE DID YOU LEARN SUCH LANGUAGE," I MUTTERED.

"I heard that," she said.

"Smart mouth for a little person."

"I am advanced for my age," she responded.

"Are you the only one?" I inquired.

"You mean in my family or in the world?"

"Well, well," I sputtered.

"Ha, got you on that one. See ya later," she twinkled.

As the brat strolled toward her home, I noticed a walk of defiance. Slump shouldered, I returned to gardening. Arghhh! Defeated by a six-year old.

This initial encounter had not gone well, proving that the wee ones are to be avoided until they are beaten down and their spirit broken by authority. In short, they are to be handled with considerable circumspection (caution) until grown.

Let me explain a bit more fully.

Children must learn respect. Adults establish certain boundaries and niceties to avoid unwanted intrusions. For example, we tell our children to close a bathroom door for privacy. We inform them about keeping off the neighbor's property. We explain about picking up after the dog when it uses another person's lawn. Most importantly, we teach them to pretend that our peculiarities (what makes us different) are not to be mentioned or laughed at. Unfortunately, all this instruction takes time and is generally ignored.

I HELD MY HEAD HIGH WHEN I RETURNED HOME FIGURING THAT EVEN A LITTLE PERSON CAN KEEP HER DIGNITY.

Rolling my toy stroller and doll up and down the street was probably best for the remainder of the day. That way, Mom and Dad could unpack by themselves. I also figured the cranky old guy would see that I was staying out of his way.

Did I already tell you that people said I am precocious (brighter than other children my age)? But, I am not always as confident as I appear.

When I went into my bedroom that evening, Dad and Mom had arranged my bed and dresser; they had also hung my old green mirror - the one Grandma gave me with an admonishment (a special warning).

"This mirror belonged to my mother's mother. It is very old. Take diligent (special) care."

Here is the deal. Sometimes, I talk to my mirror. Sometimes, my mirror answers. Shhh! Don't tell anyone or a thousand cooties will plague (pester) you.

And, here is something else.

That night, I talked with mirror. "Mom's the prettiest, Dad's the bravest, and my brother is the smartest. What am I best at?"

I knew that silence meant mirror thought I was just average. Not too skinny or heavy or smart, pretty or tall or short. Precocious or not, I felt that everyone in my family was superior. I was just the little kid. Plus, I did not have any friends in my new neighborhood yet. I would continue putting on a brave face.

DARNED HIP HURTS AGAIN.

I couldn't blame it on that kid next door, my wife, or my work. Old bones get arthritic. Being retired (when an older person stops working), my work is simply living. But, who calls it living when stuff aches?

"You got to be tough to grow old," my mother told me. I did not understand what she meant back then.

"Find something to do," Virginia ordered. "You can only read so many books, do so much gardening, and watch so much television."

That might be true. But, another truth is that concentration is hard when your eyes are a bit tired along with the rest of yourself.

THE VERY NEXT MORNING, I PRACTICALLY FLEW DOWN THE STAIRCASE.

"How can I be the best at something," I whined at breakfast?

"Practice one thing," Dad suggested. "You can become very good."

I first rode my bike faster than any child ever rode. For a while, I forgot about feeling ordinary.

I tried walking backwards. I would become the all-time fastest backward walker. Unhappily, walking backward made me dizzy.

I noticed old grumpy-face watching me from his front yard.

Then, I tried catching popcorn in my mouth. My dog, Linda, loved this game.

Again, the bad-tempered guy was peering at me through a window curtain.

"Perhaps I'll roll jelly beans with my nose, or wear a different hat every day, or catch sticks after I throw them high in the air," I suggested to mirror.

I knew what mirror would reply. "That's not so special."

"I will become the strongest girl in the world," I angrily declared.

After weeks, well really days, of push-ups, sit-ups, and bed jumping, I couldn't wait any longer.

"Look how strong I am," I told mirror.

Mirror was not impressed. I felt very small. I didn't have friends because first grade had not begun. And old sourpuss kept watching me.

SHE'S OUTSIDE AGAIN.

I figured after reading the paper I would mosey around and water my front yard plants. I recall before my father died, he warned me about being retired.

"Retired women join card and social clubs, discussion and book groups, or they simply meet for lunch," Dad had declared. "The getting together is what matters. They seem to thrive (become happy and strong) by keeping up social contacts."

"What about the guys?" I asked.

"Most of the retired men are bored. Did you notice that our neighbor washes his car every day?"

Dad told me that he was never going to become bored because he would never retire.

"If it is valuable, they pay you," he advised.

After selling a business, Dad studied to become an insurance agent. He enjoyed calling and meeting people. He never became discouraged, because the contacts, the conversations, and the opportunities to socialize were his rewards. Making money was secondary (less important). He thrived because he enjoyed being around young, old, and in-the-middle people.

Here I was enjoying the warm sun and slight breeze while spraying water onto plants that were just fine without a sprinkle.

Even as I dreamily watered the plants, my peripheral (side) vision caught sight of her. Only, she looked dejected (sad). She looked like a lost soul.

I can't explain it.

"Hey, come on over!" I yelled.

"Why were you watching me yesterday?" she yelled back. "It's creepy!"

"Never mind that!" I shouted. "Come, let me tell you something!"

When she finally approached, I talked with her as if she was a real person.

"You know, the best smells come just as rain falls. New rain delivers a special scent – a sharp, fresh odor called 'petrichor.' I looked the word up. 'Petra' means stone; 'ichor' is fluid that flows through the veins of Greek gods. So, the word describes the aroma of rain as it first dabbles (drops) onto the ground and releases earth's oils. That smell is the lifeforce of a mythical (make believe) god."

The little girl looked at me with large eyes.

"I like rain. I get to walk around with boots and an umbrella."

"So, what," I sneered.

"So, unhappy," she replied, pausing ever so softly between her words.

THAT CRUMMY OLD GUY MADE ME CRY.

And, mirror refused to help.

I was lonely, doubtful, and mirror was not cooperating. I knew school would mean stuff to do and new friends. However, I was unhappy now. How would I ever be special in my family?

When I saw Mr. Griffith watering his flowers, I decided to stay put. Why bother with that baloney head?

He kept calling me to come. I was ready for a fight as I casually strolled over to see what the jerk wanted. He began to tell me something about rain and smells and gods that I really did not understand. I tried to tell him something, anything, about rain. No sooner did the words come out of my mouth then I blurted out my sorrow. It was because of his face. I could see that he looked as miserable as me.

That's when I started to cry, silently, quietly. The gloom was in me and around me. But, it was also over him.

"BLOW YOUR NOSE IN THIS HANDKERCHIEF. DON'T GET THE SNOT ALL OVER YOURSELF. THAT'S DISGUSTING."

Naturally, she replied by calling me a mean, nasty, terrible old man. When the little girl finally recovered her composure (calm) after a good cry, I thought I might as well ask.

Asking what's wrong can be done in two ways. First, it can be offered like my phony smile. When I ask someone at a bus stop - "how are you?" - I couldn't care less. It's just a way to acknowledge (recognize) a presence. I might just as easily have said, "I see you. You are alive. The end." I am quite good at the insincere (dishonest) inquiry. For example, I might have asked the little girl, "anything wrong, sweetie?" That surely would have let the kid know that I was just not that interested.

Instead, I put some sincerity (honesty) into my voice and some care into the words. That's the other way to ask.

"Come on, come on. Spit it out. You think I have all day. What's wrong, Bailey?"

The danger is that caring words spoken sincerely might lead to an authentic (real) relationship. It might open your heart to another person and risk becoming involved. Let me tell you, disappointment might lurk (hide) inside a meaningful ask.

However, what else did I have on my calendar for today?

I CAN'T BELIEVE WHAT I SAID AFTER HE TOLD ME TO BLOW MY NOSE.

"You are a mean, nasty, terrible, old man."

Then he said, "Come on, come on. Spit it out. You think I have all day? What's wrong, Bailey?"

The geezer (old man) looked at me funny. His face was relaxed into a sad kindness despite the words. His voice sounded like he cared. That's when I felt free to tell him.

"I am just not good at anything. Everyone in my family is the best at something except me. I don't feel important. I don't have friends."

And, he remembered my name.

"MY SISTER LIKED TO RUN AND JUMP AND HANG OFF TREE LIMBS," I REMARKED.

"What happened?" Bailey asked.

"She became a terrific athlete, a cross-country runner."

"What's that?"

"Instead of running around a flat track, you and your teammates run against other teams across fields, through the woods, and even over logs."

"Do you bark?"

I ignored her foolish question, becoming quiet for a moment or two, before asking a question.

"What is one thing you like the most? Your most favorite activity in the entire world?"

"I like to run and jump, and I would love to hang off trees if I was big enough."

"Here is what I would do If I were you," I continued. "Tell your Mom to sign you up for a gymnastics program. You know, tumbling, jumping, balancing and that sort of thing. Great fun, good exercise. Know what is best of all?"

"Nope," Bailey answered.

"You are likely to make friends."

"Anything else?" she asked.

"You will be out of my sight."

"What a dope," she declared.

Then, that cute kid marched away.

AS MOM TUCKED ME INTO BED THAT EVENING, I ASKED IF SHE WOULD REGISTER ME FOR GYMNASTIC CLASSES.

"Well, if that is what you want, sure."

"Just me," I mumbled as the tiredness took over. "Something special for me."

The next morning, I excitedly explained to mirror that I would be the only one in the family who would be taking gymnastics.

Mirror's reaction, "Oh, hum."

Every weekday afternoon, I attended a gymnastics class with other children. We laughed as we learned. I even went to training on Saturdays. School started, but I continued practicing forward and backward somersaults, cartwheels, headstands, and even handsprings. At night, I was too weary to chat with mirror.

On Sundays, I began to visit old grouchy-pants. He seemed glad to see me. We had chocolate milk and graham crackers at his kitchen table. He told me about his life, his work, and his family. I told him about gymnastics, my new friends, and my family. We talked about Greek gods and something called sarcasm. That's when you pretend to say something pleasant, but it's really mean. He's excellent at sarcasm.

"So, what are you learning from the gymnastics experience?" Mr. Griffith asked.

"All sorts of acrobatic stuff," I answered.

"No, no. I know you are learning tumbling. What I am asking is what did you learn?"

I thought for a few moments about what he meant. Then, it clicked.

"I learned about figuring out what I want and asking."

"Anything else?" he wondered.

"My gym buddies make me feel better about myself. But, I wonder whether I will ever feel just right."

One Sunday, I invited Mr. Griffith to parents' night at the gym. I told him I would be showing off my new skills.

"Break a leg," he said with a smile.

"Huh?" Had he changed back to the grouchy guy?

"Break a leg is an actor's expression," he explained. "It means just the opposite. Something like good luck. But, wishing somebody who is about to perform good luck is said to bring bad luck. So, you say a mean thing, it's a joke to bring the person good luck."

"Ok, if you say so. Just be there or be a square."

"THE LITTLE GIRL WANTS ME TO SEE HER PERFORM ON PARENTS' NIGHT, AMAZING," I TOLD VIRGINIA.

"Come on," I nagged. "Let's see if the squirt can do anything."

IT WAS FINALLY TIME TO DEMONSTRATE MY SKILLS.

Students would perform in front of their families. I would show off for my family. I hoped Mr. Griffith might be watching.

For breakfast, Dad fixed his special pancakes. I could tell he was pleased. Mom packed a note with my lunch that read, 'Can't wait for the show. Love, Mom.'

At supper, I was so excited about the performance that I wasn't even hungry!

Then we were at the gym. When it was my turn, I heard someone shout, "That little girl's my friend!" It was old man Griffith.

I had rehearsed over and over. I completed my routine almost perfectly.

Of course, Mom, Dad, and my brother said that I did great. Mr. Griffith came up after the show. He said, "You look happy. I'm glad for you."

For some reason, tears . . . just little ones . . . rolled down the corners of my eyes. But, I didn't let that old guy see so that he wouldn't think I had gone mushy on him.

Later that night, I stood in front of mirror.

"I may not be the strongest girl," I told mirror. "But, I did well today."
I didn't wait for mirror's response before climbing into bed.

Jack and the Titan

"The spots crawl."

After spending Sunday afternoon hanging wallpaper behind Paul's headboard, he was letting me know that he couldn't sleep because the colorful rows of blue, brown, orange, and green circles frightened him.

"As soon as you turn off the light," he whimpered.

"How about a story?" I offered.

"Sure."

Outfitted in white pajamas imprinted with cartoon dinosaurs, my sad-sack son sat on his bed where I joined him.

A NIGHTTIME STORY

"Once upon a time," I began, "a lady baked a gingerbread cookie in the shape of a small boy. When fully baked, the lady opened the oven. Out jumped a spritely (lively) gingerbread boy. Townspeople from all around tried to catch him. He ran so . . ."

"Stop," Paul ordered. "Tell me about Jack."

Because Jack and the Beanstalk had become his favorite story, I started over.

"Once upon a time, a boy disobeys his mother, runs away, steals a magic harp, kills the harp's owner, and lives happily ever after."

"Just tell the story, please," Paul asked.

"After Jack's father died from unknown causes, Jack and his mother tried with little success to maintain their farmette."

"What's a farmette?" Paul questioned.

"A small farm. Really, all they had was a patch of a garden next to their tiny cottage, a drafty barn, a couple of chickens, and a cow."

"Did the cow have a name?"

"No. Farmers don't like to give names to their animals. Except for pets, of course."

"The magic beans. Come on," Paul implored.

"Jack's mom, Minnie, told him to take the cow to market."

She said, "I know you are only a youngster, but I am depending on you to sell our cow for a decent price. Bring the money home. We need food, clothes, and seed for next year's crop."

"Did he do what she told him?" Paul asked.

"Jack walked the no-name cow to the local market while playing his worn harmonica to make the trip a bit more pleasant. He was about to strike a deal with the cow buyer when an old, scrawny man sidled (crept) up and whispered in his ear."

"Beans," Paul blurted.

"'I got some beans right here, sonny,' the fellow revealed. "Some magic beans."

"With that, the aged one held a few withered pods in the palm of his weathered hand."

"You will be in beans forever," he assured the boy. "Bushels of beans. Just plant and reap (harvest)."

"So, Jack traded, right?"

"I am afraid that greed might have influenced Jack," I replied.

"I thought he traded, Dad. You know, a cow for a few beans. He plants beans, a giant stalk, Jack climbs and steals a magic harp from a giant, runs fast with the giant following, he cuts the stalk and kills the giant, and everyone lives happily ever after."

Paul had rushed the Little Golden Book version in one hurried breath. When he finally paused, I continued.

THE ADVENTURE BEGINS

"After Jack sold the cow, he pocketed his money. On the way out of town, Jack spotted the old guy fast asleep on the side of the road. The guy's head was resting on an old canvas sack. He slept under a worn overcoat, legs were curled, arms were flopped forward, and he was snoring."

"What did Jack do?"

"He stole the beans. Took them right out of the old man's overcoat pocket. When Jack returned home, he gave Minnie the money. Later, he snuck outside and planted the beans in their garden. His stomach felt a bit upset, perhaps he had mistreated the old guy. Oh well, Jack decided to sleep off the belly ache."

"What then?"

"Overnight, the beans sprouted. Each bean stalk twisted like a lanyard around the other stalks to form a thick trunk that stretched up and up toward the clouds with plenty of footholds and handholds for climbing."

I could see Paul picturing the stalk in his imagination.

"Before Minnie woke, when the sky was barely light, Jack scrambled off his bed. He quickly used the outhouse (outdoor toilet), dressed in the only pair of pants and shirt he owned, tossed his harmonica into a pocket, and ran barefoot to see whether the beans had produced anything."

"He saw the stalk, right," Paul cried. "How could he miss it?"

"Jack was taken aback (surprised). He stretched his neck backward while gazing upward with his mouth open and his eyes wide."

"And he started to climb right away, right?"

"Do you want him to begin his journey immediately, or gather up some food and equipment first? How about his mother? Tell her, or wait until his possible return? Perhaps leave her a note. 'Mom, up the stalk. Be back whenever, Jack.'"

"Hold it. You said, possible return. Does he get back safely?"

"Jack was an impetuous (reckless) kid. Without a care, he placed one foot on the stalk and started the climb upward. It would be well over three days of persistent (determined) foraging (living off the land) before he arrived at a solid surface."

"Wait a minute! Hold on. No sleep or food or . . ."

"During the long journey, Jack stopped for respites (breaks). There were large outcrops of giant bean pods on which he could rest. In fact, he sometimes fell asleep right on a shell. Fortunately, by sheer perseverance (insistence), he broke open pods to munch on the succulent (luscious) bean insides. They melted in his mouth, supplying him with nourishment (food and water)."

"Anything else?"

"Well, I did not want to mention this aspect (part). But, sometimes young Jack took a bathroom break . . ."

"I don't really want to hear about that part."

JACK MEETS THE GIANT

"Upon reaching solid ground, Jack quickly jumped onto a path. He was curious about the towering castle set off in the distance. As he approached, the castle's massive (enormous) double doors swung open. Before him stood a gargantuan (huge) man. He stood eight feet in height, with a large body, and with colossal (really large) shoulders, neck, head, and hands."

"Was Jack scared?"

"Jack was frozen with fright. If his feet were not stuck to the floor, if he could move an arm, a leg, or even a finger, he would have fled."

"What happened next?" Paul asked.

"Seeing the giant's glowering visage (mean face) multiplied Jack's fears."

"Are you afraid sometimes, Dad?"

"I would have been afraid of that giant! Of course, sometimes when its necessary, we do things we don't believe we can do. Lots of times we need others to help. Mostly, I talk to someone to try and lower my fears. Saying my fear out loud helps."

I noticed Paul considering what I just revealed. "Shall I go on with the story," I asked?

"I'm glad I told you I'm scared of the circles," Paul softly confessed.

"I receive so few visitors," the oversized man declared with an unsettling grimace (scowl). "You see, I am the last of my Titan race. Lacking companionship, all who wander into my domain (area) are welcome. The last human who stayed with me, unfortunately, left in some haste. Before departing, he grabbed some beans, some magic beans. Would you know something about that?"

"Jack looked first at his feet, then off to the side, and finally into the air."

"I just found myself here," Jack finally replied.

"Why was Jack lying?" Paul asked.

"What do you think?"

"He probably did not want to tell the giant that he stole the old man's beans."

"Yup. Jack was stuck. If he told the giant the truth, the Titan might become terribly angry with the little thief. If he continued to lie, things might become worse should the giant discover Jack's deceptions (lies)."

"Oh boy, you do one little wrong thing," Paul whined, "and, you get deep in trouble."

WHAT'S A BOY TO DO?

"Fortunately, Jack did not have to decide at that moment how he might further explain his presence. The titan showed him a bedroom and invited Jack to dine with him after resting. As soon as the giant left, Jack tiptoed from his room and carefully began investigating."

"What did he see?"

"Oh, the usual stuff. Jewels lying about, bones scattered in the pantry, and a golden harp leaning against a wall in the great room. The harp was quietly singing to itself."

"I bet Jack took the harp and ran."

"Jack approached the harp and introduced himself. He asked the harp whether she knew what the giant might do with him."

"Titan is a lovely man for those who ain't his meals," the enchanted harp sang. "But, if I was a little lad, I'd take off on my wheels."

"Hello again." The titan jovially (merrily) announced his presence as he stomped into the great room. "It's time to eat. I'm famished (hungry)."

"Yes, I bet you are starving," Jack mumbled.

"Please, follow me to the eating area."

"Oddly, the table was bare. The giant sat at one end of the table; Jack sat at the other end. Before sitting, the titan had brushed the dirt from Jack's shoulders and arms with a couple of swipes of his enormous hands. As he cleaned Jack's garments (clothes), the titan had licked his lips in anticipation."

"Pardon me," Jack inquired. "Where's the food?"

"Close your eyes and imagine what you might like to eat," the giant suggested. "What would fill you with pleasure. Don't forget desert."

"Oh, oh," Paul exclaimed. "I kind of know what's coming next."

"Jack's hunger overcame his fear. He imagined a porridge thick with molasses. Along with a couple of buttered potatoes, he thought of how a slice of juicy roast beef would taste alongside candied apples and a bit of blueberry pie. A drink of milk would be just right to complete his repast (meal)."

"What happened next? Did the giant eat him for real?"

"Jack's imaginary meal wondrously relieved his need to eat, but his stress (anxiety) over the giant's intention (purpose) returned."

"Come on, come on," Paul urged.

"As Jack opened his eyes, the table remained bare. The titan remained seated. Time seemed to have stopped. The castle seemed too quiet except for the pounding Jack heard in his ears."

"And?"

JACK SKEDADDLES (GETS AWAY)

"I let the old guy go with some magic beans," the titan admitted.

"What about fee-fie-fo-fum, I smell the blood of an Englishman? What about be he alive or be he dead, I'll grind his bones to make my bread?" Jack asked.

"I was never going to grind up that skinny old man's bones," the giant continued. "He had nary (hardly) a scrap worth devouring (eating). I used him to lure (tempt) some tastier morsels (food) to my home. I knew that tramp would palm off those beans to some unsuspecting person. I must say, I'm a bit disappointed that you are so small."

"Suddenly, everything that had occurred became clear to Jack. This was his moment of clarity (clearness). A moment when his guts and brains met in perfect agreement."

"Dad, what are you talking about?"

"In a flash, in an instant, in less time than it takes to blink twice, Jack understood why his stomach had been feeling queasy ever since he stole the beans. All he had to do was avoid being eaten alive, get back home, and make things right with that homeless man."

"I admit that what I did was wrong," Jack declared.

"Come on, Dad, is he going to talk or run?"

"But," Jack continued, "that doesn't mean I have to put up with a big lug who has a hankering for a small fry!"

"As the giant reached one of his large paws right across the table, intending to grab the boy, Jack deftly (skillfully) jumped off his chair, ran down a long hallway, leaped into the great room, and . . ."

"How about the golden harp?" Paul asked.

"Oh, I forgot. I am not going to insult your intelligence by claiming that a small boy might be sufficiently strong to haul a harp out of a castle and down a bean stalk, much less a yelling harp constructed of gold."

"So, no harp. Get on with it, please," Paul requested.

"As Jack leaped through the great room, the harp clamored (shouted) about Jack being a tasty snack. Even while Jack heard the lumbering giant, he spotted a shiny harmonica sitting by itself on a bejeweled table."

"Stop!" yelled the harmonica. "Please, take me with you. I am sort of magical. You will be able to play me about as good as a harmonica can be played. And, you will take me far away from that ogre who can't carry a tune in a pail (non-musical). Please, please. By the way, I can help you escape."

"Did he take the harmonica?" Paul wondered.

"Ahh. Jack had learned his lesson. He deftly (quickly) switched his harmonica for the giant's harmonica. Sort of a fair trade, Jack thought. After all, that boy-eating bully was going to dispose of me in a most unpleasant way. And, this time I am trying to save my life."

CONCLUSION

"Please go ahead, I'm getting kind of sleepy," Paul yawned.

"His new harmonica turned out to be a valuable partner. Singing in sharps, flats, and natural notes, the mouth organ directed Jack toward an escape route that soon returned him to the stalk."

"And he spent another three days getting back home?" Paul sputtered.

"Jack found descending (going down) much quicker than ascension (going up)."

"Was the titan following?" Paul asked.

"The giant was disappointed. He would have to wait for another visitor on another day. It was too much effort for too little reward to attempt a recapture of that little rascal, Jack."

"What happened next," Paul asked?

"As soon as Jack touched a foot to his home land, the bean stalk withered and fell to earth. Jack had to move lively to avoid being smothered by the vines and pods. His mother grabbed Jack and hugged and hugged him. Jack advised her that they needed to gather the pods and grow their own plants. Soon afterwards, Jack and his mother opened a small stand and sold the tastiest bean pies. Their successful pies provided money for them to live comfortably for the rest of their lives."

"Is that it?" Paul asked.

"Well, just a few odds and ends to resolve," I explained. "After making enough money so that Jack could take some time away from the business, he rambled (roamed) around until he found the old man from whom he had taken the beans. He invited him to live with the family. The homeless man immediately agreed. Afterwards, Jack kept himself busy playing harmonica with other musicians from the village. Turned out, the old fellow had a fetching (attractive) voice. So, he joined the band."

"Oh, Dad, I'm really tired. But, I'm still afraid. Those spots might start moving again. I guess I'm not as brave as Jack."

"When you told me that you fear the wallpaper after I spent all afternoon hanging it, that was darn brave. How about if you sleep in our bed tonight. Any other ideas?"

"Could we remove that wallpaper," Paul suggested?

"When I come home from work tomorrow, we'll take it off together."

"How about we get me a harmonica and we plant some beans and . . ." Paul's voice trailed off as he fell asleep in his own bed.

Book 2

Anthony's Story

CHAPTER 1

"Tony," my teacher asked, "what are you doing? Anthony Rossi, look up!"

Other students tittered, relieved not to be her target.

"Sorry, Miss Judge."

"What have you got there? There, in your lap."

"Nothing."

"You were reading again. Put it away. Now!"

I fumbled *Twenty Thousand Leagues Under the Sea* onto the floor and heard more laughter as I picked up the book.

Fifth grade had not turned out any better than previous school years. The teachers had rules; I had other interests. My face revealed gray eyes, black hair bristling crew cut style, and a prominent nose. Relatives told me that I looked more rugged – even craggy – than handsome. Going on eleven, my sunken cheeks made me appear gaunt. Although I gave the impression of being tough, I daydreamed about how I might enjoy adventures like those undertaken by the characters from my books.

Tired of living in a low-rise apartment building nestled among a hodge-podge of similar brick and stone structures in Newark's Ironbound district, I hated my run-down neighborhood crammed with Irish, Jewish, Italian, and Portuguese immigrants struggling to make a living among previously settled Germans and southern blacks. Feeling sorry for the despair caused to everyone I knew by the never-ending depression, I frequently recalled a poem my teacher shared with the class.

In the town of many riches
Bringing sufferings and many promises
Still, no help wanted, no help wanted.
Men walk the streets in rags
Starving and begging for cash;
Morristown, Oh Morristown what shame is upon us?
Still, no help wanted, no help wanted.

ANTHONY DERUGGIERO, 1931

During the remainder of the school day, I barely heard the muffled sounds of assignments given. I paid scant attention to classroom activities. With the final bell, I walked swiftly from school to my branch library where I might finish the book. This space was oddly located above a fire house whose siren periodically startled readers from their reveries. I didn't care. Within that second-floor reading room, I settled onto a comfy chair feeling safe until it was time to walk home for chores and dinner.

"Hey that blind guy just picked up a nickel!" a guy angrily hollered.

I watched transfixed while several men started punching and kicking a pitifully dressed beggar. His cane went flying in one direction, his dark glasses in another.

"People will do about anything when they're hungry," my father once told me.

Would I ever escape the squalor?

CHAPTER 2

"Anthony, venite a mangiare!" Mama called. Come and eat.

Sitting at the kitchen table with his dad and older brother, I took up some pasta from my bowl with a soup spoon in my left hand and a fork in my right. After a quick twirl, pasta was positioned on my fork with just enough sauce to be slurped without making too much of a mess. Mama sat after all the plates were full.

I wanted to tell the family during dinner how the Nautilus was powered electrically. Did they know Davy Crocket had learned to shoot squirrels as a kid? I yearned to inform them about how the Italian word for sugar, zucchero, derived from the Arabic sukkar, which means intoxicating.

However, I ate in silence except for sounds of food being chomped, slurped, and swallowed. At day's end, the family was exhausted. No energy was left for casual conversation. Plus, the apartment was often too cold or too hot, which made everyone grumpy.

Always short on money, dad hauled pallets at a warehouse when he could get a day's hire. My older brother worked as a helper traveling by truck from one small grocery store to another collecting used wooden bushels and cardboard egg cartons for salvage. Mama remained home shopping, cooking, and cleaning. She began a beauty salon business in our apartment by resuming a skill learned before marriage.

I knew that in a few years education would likely be abandoned to assist the family. For now, I made a dollar or two each week doing odd jobs for the building superintendent. During the winter, I fed coal into the furnace. In the summer, I hauled ice up worn staircases for several families. Once a week, I wheeled garbage dumpsters from the basement to the curb.

CHAPTER 3

As I ate, I flashed back to when I watched Mama prepare dinner.

She always started with a little olive oil in a large frying pan. "Appena un po." Just a bit.

She sliced and diced green peppers and yellow onions, which she tossed into the pan.

"Deliziosa!"

While the peppers and onions began to cook on a low flame, Mama washed, cut up, and added mushrooms. Finally, she peeled and sliced garlic cloves that she also threw into the pan. She turned up the flame and Joe marveled at the ease with which she flipped the pan back and forth while moving the ingredients around with her large, wooden spoon. As she cooked, Ma commented about what Papa disliked.

"Egli non è come lo zucchero nel suo sugo." He don't like sugar in his sauce.

"Senza zucchero." No sugar.

"Egli non piace un sacco di sale e di pepe." He don't like lots of salt and pepper.

When her vegetables sizzled to translucence, Mama scrapped them into an oversized pot to which she had added lots of home-made tomato sauce; bunches of chopped oregano and basil; a shake of salt and black pepper; two bay leaves; and, finally, a pinch or two of thyme. With the large wooden spoon, she would take occasional tastes.

"Perfetto!"

I knew that Mama would now start on the meatballs. She let him pan fry the sausage.

"Make sure the sausage don't burn, Anthony. You turn it a couple times in the pan when it sizzles. Then throw it in, huh!"

"Certo, Ma."

While the sausage began to brown in the frying pan, Mama worked some eggs and bread crumbs into a bowl with ground beef. She began forming little meatballs with her reddened, wet hands. As Mama shaped the meatballs, she threw them into a lightly, olive-oiled frying pan. She rotated between making meatballs and moving them around the pan with her wooden spoon.

"Essa ha per sear tutto intorno. Proprio così." It has to sear all around. Just so.

Once the sausage and then the meatballs were all-around browned, they were added to the big pot.

After partially covering the pot, she let it simmer hour after hour to thicken and capture the flavors.

I thought about other dishes. He recalled how Mama pounded veal for scaloppini, braised cut up chicken in her frying pan for chicken cacciatore; and worked thick dough on a wooden board for Sicilian pizza.

For tonight, twist and slurp. Yummy.

CHAPTER 4

Ma said that I had to start learning a trade, something I could depend on for a living. First, I just swept hair from the living room floor that she had covered with a sheet of linoleum. Once I collected a pile, I picked up the hair with my hands and dumped it into the garbage can.

One day, Ma ordered me to help with a customer.

"Estrarre i rulli. Non ti preoccupare, queste signore sono dure." Pull out the rollers. Don't worry, these ladies are tough.

Before the next day's customer arrived, Ma offered me some instruction.

"First shampoo the head. Nobody likes working on a smelly head. Shampooing makes the hair cutting easier."

Once I mastered shampooing, I learned to pin and roll.

"I cut, you pin and put on the rollers."

"How do you know what hairstyle to do?" I asked.

"Listen to what the customer wants. Then look at her face, her neck, her age, what needs to be covered, what should be shown. Give her something like what she wants. But, style with your hands to make her look good. Well, some of these old bags can only look so, so. But, you either got the style in your hands or forget it. We'll make you a plumber or something."

"How do you know if you did good?" I wondered.

"Se non torneranno, non hai fatto cosi bene." If they don't come back, you did not do so good.

I liked styling. I preferred reading.

CHAPTER 5

During the next couple of years, my brother left to work with the Works Progress Administration repairing roads. Then, Dad passed away. I remained home completing school, snatching reading time, and honing hair-styling skills. High school was nearing completion when Ma sat me down.

"Tony, I don't want to make your life for you. But, I am too old to make a living. You gotta quit school."

After our talk, I wondered. Would I follow Shakespeare's advice and listen to what I wanted?

This above all: to thine own self be true,
And it must follow, as the night the day,
Thou canst not then be false to any man.
Farewell, my blessing season this in thee!

Or, would Milton's warning about the danger of defying a parent carry the day?

OF Mans First Disobedience, and the Fruit
Of that Forbidden Tree, whose mortal tast
Brought Death into the World, and all our woe,
With loss of *Eden*, till one greater Man
Restore us, and regain the blissful Seat,
Sing Heav'nly Muse,

CHAPTER 6

We lived comfortably. I had escaped the dreadful poverty of my youth by becoming the successful Mr. Anthony, haute coiffure. The reading, the daydreaming, the playing with ideas and language were lost to practicality.

"Frankie, sweep up the hair on the floor," I told my eleven-year old son.

"Sure, Dad."

After a few weeks of getting the boy acclimated to the rhythm of a fast-paced beauty salon, I called him over to where I was working on a customer who had just come out from under her hairdryer.

"Take out the rollers, Frank."

He was awfully clumsy trying ever so carefully to remove them one by one.

Frank enjoyed learning how to make pasta and meatballs with real Italian sauce. We joked and cooked. It was not so much fun when he tried hairdressing.

"These ladies are tough. Watch."

After I grabbed a bunch of the rollers from front to back – off they came.

Frank was not only unable to quickly remove the hair rollers, he had no ability to cut, comb, or visualize a hairstyle. The artistry was not in his hands.

Later, while we drove home, I asked him a serious question.

"Frankie, what is it you might want to do?"

"I like history. Did you know that the name Christopher Columbus probably means Christ's dove? Ironic, considering what a murderer he was when Christianizing native people in the New World."

"Thank goodness," I muttered under my breath.

Jeffrey's Story

AT MOM'S KNEE

Mom was not a patient person. She was nimble in accomplishing tasks, forthright in expressing opinions, and intolerant of those who were too slow. She did not look down upon people who were not as quick. She would simply rather do it herself. The frustration of watching someone work or think in slow motion was excruciating. Her child emulated her personality, a personality that demanded perfection.

"Jeffrey, don't wait around to be told about a task. See it, do it!" she barked.

And, doing it meant accomplishing the task correctly and completely without any thanks. No appreciation because what was done needed to be done, needed to be done the right way. I remember most of the framed advisements posted on our bathroom walls. After all, I was a trapped audience.

Patience is a tree whose root is bitter, but its fruit is very sweet.

The thing that goes the farthest towards making life worthwhile
That cost the least and does the most is just a pleasant smile.

Let me be a little kinder, let me be a little blinder / To the faults of those about me. / Let me be when I am weary, just a little bit more cheery.

As I got older, I wondered at the irony of her wall hangings.
Mom also displayed a poem that I did find endearing.

The Night has a thousand eyes,
And the day but one;
Yet the light of the whole world dies
At set of sun.
The mind has a thousand eyes,
And the heart but one;
Yet the light of a whole life dies
When love is done.

TWO KINDS OF PEOPLE, KIND AND UNKIND

"Hi Jeff, want to come over to a party tonight?" Stanley asked.

What an unusual call. We were both thirteen – almost fourteen. We attended the same school. He lived a couple of blocks away. But, we lived in separate galaxies. Stanley was handsome, athletic, and outgoing. He had oodles of friends. I was none of the above. Looking back, it is obvious what happened. Stanley was Tessie's son; Tessie was Mom's good friend.

When I arrived, Stanley was friendly. His friends talked with me as if I mattered. After a while, we were invited to participate in a game. One person at a time was invited to go downstairs into the basement rec room. I was the last person invited. When I went downstairs, the kissing game was well underway with boy, girl, boy, girl lined up. When the person at the head of the line asked a question, the person directly behind answered and received a kiss. Instead of a kiss when my turn came, I received a slap. Everyone laughed. The party resumed with soft drinks and snacks as I eased my way out of the door and started to walk home.

"Jeffrey, you need some friends. Some place where you can meet other people your age."

"I'm doing well in school, Mom." I replied.

That was partially true. My grades were excellent, my social skills were the pits. I could be a bit arrogant, perhaps a tad intolerant.

"That is not the point." Mom persisted. "How about if you try something I arranged? If you don't like it, just stop."

Mom was forceful and logical. I knew from experience. Take the time I was sneaking smokes. She found a couple of loose cigarettes in my sock drawer.

"You do know that smoking causes deadly diseases. Plus, it's an expensive and smelly habit."

"Yes," I answered guiltily.

"I will not waste time trying to convince you to stop smoking. You will do it with or without my permission. Let's agree to two things. First, you may not smoke in the house. Secondly, when you finish high school, I will not say a word if you still want to smoke – outside."

Mothers can be so clever. She figured that by the time I finished high school, some common sense would lead me away from smoking. And, she was right. I never smoked again.

I sometimes wonder what happens if parents always win.

"What did you arrange?" I asked.

"A group of young people meet at the Ethical Culture Society weekly. That's the place I've been attending on Sunday mornings. It's a religious organization where we meet to talk and learn. But, this group meets on Thursday evenings. It's just teens, no adults."

"How do I get there, walk?"

"No. Mr. Rapp will pick you up. His daughter will be attending. He will drop you back home."

When Mr. Rapp arrived that first Thursday driving his Morris Minor, Doris was squeezed into the small back seat. I sat in the bucket seat next to him. It was pouring rain. Despite the blower going at its full whirl, the air remained humid, increasing my unease because we were uncomfortably close in this midget of a car. Mr. Rapp was doing his best to present a jovial presence to his sullen riders while remaining glued to the front windshield.

"You both go on in," Mr. Rapp advised. "I'm getting some coffee and pie at a diner. I'll pick you up later."

As soon as we walked into the Society's modest, older home remodeled into a meeting place, an older girl greeted us.

"Hi Doris! Hi, Jeff! I'm Susan. Glad you could make it."

THE GROUP

Obviously, she was going out of her way to pretend niceness.

"We sit around this living area," Susan explained. "You sit where you want, like the couch, the old stuffed chair, or on one of the folding chairs. We introduce ourselves. You'll see."

After everyone sat, the chit-chat slowly stopped.

"Hi all. I'm Susan. I'm glad to be here. For our newcomers' sake, we talk about the evening's subject. Or, you can just listen if you prefer. I get to moderate tonight. We take a break for drinks and snacks after I sense we are kind of worn out. Then, we gather again and talk about whatever we want. We always stop at nine, so parents don't get too upset on a school night."

That first evening, I listened. Attenders ranged the teen gamut. The mix was about an equal number of boys and girls. The discussion centered around bullying. Have we experienced getting bullied? How do we react? What can we do if we are picked on? Do we have an obligation toward others?

I was amazed by the discussion that extended into physical and mental abuse. They seemed smart. Several group members talked openly of bad experiences. Some talked about asking friends to intercede. We agreed that speaking up for ourselves was good. But when you feel alone, it is oh, so difficult.

Before we broke up, we formed into groups of two or three. Doris, Susan, and I ended up together.

"What do you think is a good date?" Susan asked.

"Two people clicking," I suggested.

"Doris?" Susan asked.

"A succulent fruit."

Doris seem pleased when Susan and I laughed.

"How was it, guys?" Mr. Rapp asked as soon as we squeezed into his car.

"OK, I guess," I mumbled.

"I guess we'll get used to it," Doris said. "I hope you decide to try the meeting again, Jeff."

When they dropped me off, I was glad of two things. First, the rain had ended so that the return ride was not so harrowing. Secondly, nobody tried to make fun of me. I guess I'll go again.

WHAT DO YOU BELIEVE?

At our next meeting, the discussion was led by Chris. This time, I would contribute. I was beginning to like these people.

"We're going to talk about what we believe. Again, no right or wrong comments. Does someone want to begin?"

"Like Woody Allen," I jumped in, "I believe that there's an overall intelligence in the universe, except for certain parts of New Jersey."

I waited for the laughter that did not arrive.

"Jeff, what <u>do you</u> believe?" Chris persevered with some force behind his question.

"I'm not sure," I replied. "I know what I do not believe. I do not believe that people ought to harm each other. I do not believe that I should be the butt of someone's joke. I don't believe that just because I like to read and make sure things are done correctly, I should be treated as an outcast."

Everyone was quiet for a moment.

"Thanks, Jeff," Chris said. "Anyone else?"

"Well, Felix Adler thought that by making others key to our lives, we find purpose and value for ourselves," Samar contributed.

"Who was this Felix Adler guy?" I asked.

"He was the founder of our Ethical Culture societies," Susan explained.

"But, some people are difficult," Doris noted.

"And, interacting with them is tough. Talk about your conflict. Plus, we like to be independent," Gary offered.

"What a mess," Doris sighed.

"The problem," Samar continued, "happens when we realize that we depend on others. That's counter to our desire for independence. Unfortunately, when we make others important, we can't entirely avoid conflict."

"Kind of a balancing act," I suggested.

"A balancing act for sure," Samar said. "Maybe, the best we can hope for is that we recognize our need for other people while also paying attention to our own needs."

"Adler did not claim that his philosophy eliminates conflict," Chris said. "It offers a way to address feelings of isolation and powerlessness by claiming individual worth while acknowledging our reliance on others."

"That sounds like a book. Where did you learn all this stuff?" I asked.

"Reading and listening at Platform meetings," Samar replied.

"Plus, Saul is a terrific Society Leader, you know like a minister, who explains ideas without telling us how to think or act," Susan added.

From there, the discussion veered toward making right choices and right relationships.

"How do you know what's right?" I asked.

"We can't expect someone else to be responsible for our decisions," Chris said. "How we decide to act is entirely up to us. But, Saul's idea is that blaming others avoids responsibility. It also gives them power over us."

"How do you put these ideas into action?" I wondered aloud.

"Let's pretend that you act in a certain way that is no longer helpful," Samar suggested.

"Like biting my nails?" Doris asked.

"Sure, why not?" Samar replied. "You began to nail-bite maybe to relieve stress as a little kid. Now, you continue out of force of habit."

"The most powerful force in the universe," I offered.

This time my new friends laughed.

"I get trying to change something that is no longer valuable," I said. "In fact, a habit might be negative like avoiding telling people what I believe because I was made fun of. Or, it might be positive like putting my wallet where I can find it in the morning. What I don't understand is how I know if my choices and relationships are right."

"Did you use your rational mind and touch base with your emotions?" Samar asked. "Are you following what you want? Are you bringing out the best in others?"

RIDE HOME

"You guys OK?" Mr. Rapp asked after we settled into his miniature car.

"Sure, Dad. A serious discussion tonight. Lots to chew on," Doris replied.

"I am still thinking about changing behavior," I said.

"Well," Mr. Rapp said. "Do you want a middle-aged guy's point of view?"

"Why not," I answered.

"Oh, oh," Doris said with a slight laugh, "now you've opened the door to diarrhea of the mouth as Mom calls it."

Mr. Rapp seemed unperturbed by his daughter's salty talk.

"Changing behavior sometimes requires acting as if we are who we want to be," he continued.

"I don't exactly get it," I told him.

"First, think about whether you only act well toward another person if you want something. Rather than bartering to win, what if you permit the magic to occur by listening carefully to what another person might be asking. Sometimes, the ask is indirect. The person might be simply wanting acknowledgement that something painful happened. This is how we start becoming who we want to be – we first act as if we care."

"Do we abandon our needs?" I asked.

"Not at all," Mr. Rapp replied. "We negotiate because if we don't get what we need, we become resentful."

"Are you saying we should pretend to be oh, so nice? Isn't that being a phony?" Doris asked.

"When people are friendly and kind to me, I like to respond in kind," Mr. Rapp answered.

"I think I get it," I jumped in. "Maybe we start off acting. Kind of like practicing a skill. When the response is positive, we do it again. Only, the next time caring is a bit easier and more honest."

Doris was quiet for a moment. Then she wistfully said, "an island of one gets very lonely."

"What happens," I asked, "if your mom insists that she is always right?"

"Do you like vanilla or chocolate ice cream?" Mr. Rapp questioned.

"I like vanilla," I replied.

"No, that is just not correct. Most people like chocolate," he said.

"Well, I get to pick my own flavor," I responded indignantly. "The ice cream I prefer is vanilla."

"You got it, Jeff. We get to choose what we like, what we believe, and how we want to live. Otherwise, we end up eating the ice cream our mom prefers."

"Is there a name for what you are describing?" I wondered.

"Yup," Mr. Rapp replied. "It's called having a little backbone."

ANOTHER THURSDAY AND THE PARADOX GUY

Gary started us off with a question. "What subject would interest you for this discussion?"

"Paradox," Jorge immediately shouted.

That caught everybody's attention because Jorge is rather shy.

"What do you mean?" Tiana asked. "Could you explain?"

Everyone stopped fidgeting and turned to listen. Having garnered the spotlight, the paradox guy was suddenly speechless. Perhaps he was embarrassed by the sudden attention. Perhaps a synapse having fired, shut off. Perhaps he blurted a first thought with nothing behind it. Just a word. After a quiet moment, our conversation moved on to another topic for discussion.

I liked Jorge's suggestion.

I wonder about the paradox that is us. Why do we treat each other decently, yet laugh at the slapstick comedy of a pratfall? How can we crave equilibrium, yet continuously place stress on ourselves? Why do we demand rational decisions, but gravitate toward the eccentric? We feel sorry for the less fortunate while clutching dearly to what we have. We cuddle a baby one moment, and berate someone for a simple mistake the next.

I wish I had responded to Jorge's suggestion by saying that people are a complex bundle of contradictions. We are capable of incredible kindness and stupefying cruelty. We exhibit weakness, and demand perfection. We act rationally except when we are unpredictable. We aspire to greatness, and act with pettiness. I recall appreciating Hamlet's exasperation with the contradiction between our potential and our reality.

> What a piece of work is a man, how noble in reason, how infinite in faculties, in form and moving how express and admirable, in action how like an angel, in apprehension how like a god! the beauty of the world, the paragon of animals—and yet, to me, what is this quintessence of dust?

JEFF, IS IT?

As I was getting ready to leave, the Society's Leader walked past me. I decided to take a chance. After all, Mr. Rapp had not yet returned.

I explained what occurred with Jorge.

"Jeff, is it?"

"Yes, sir," I tentatively replied.

"Just call me Saul, please."

"OK, Saul."

"What happened, I think, is that you felt what psychologists call empathy. You experienced what it might have felt like to have been Jorge after he was startled by all the attention."

"But, I was not him."

"Unintentionally, you were realizing what he might have felt. Empathy is very positive, very powerful."

"If it is so positive, why am I feeling bad about what happened?"

"Had you spoken up about some of the things you were thinking about paradox, how might Jorge have reacted to your remarks?"

"I think he would have felt pretty darn good. It would have shown him that at least somebody in the group was trying to understand."

"Yes. What you are now describing is called affirmation. You might have affirmed that his request had merit. At the least, you would have acknowledged him. Sometimes, that is all we want."

"Oh! I guess I blew it, huh?" I groaned.

"One thing about being alive is that we sometimes get to try again," Saul said. "Opportunities to exhibit empathy and affirmation will arise. You will be better prepared next time to listen to your inner voice. Then, you will likely act and feel better about yourself."

"That's good," I said.

"By the way, I like that you noticed something was wrong with how the group left Jorge feeling unappreciated."

"Thanks," I said.

"Here's something else you might want to keep in mind. If you decide to show someone empathy, consider that you are just guessing about how that person might be feeling. By asking, the person might agree with your understanding of the situation, but most likely you will get a better description about their feelings. Whether you get it right the first time or not is unimportant. What matters is whether you reach out to ask by checking with the person."

"That makes lots of sense. I can see why the kids like you."

"Ahh, flattery will get you everywhere," he joked. "But it's good to hear genuine compliments. It makes me feel appreciated."

"The mind has a thousand eyes. Yet the light of a whole life dies, when caring is done," I mumbled.

"What was that?" Saul asked.

"Oh, nothing. See you around."

A TALK

The following Sunday, I attended my first Sunday morning service at the Ethical Society. After a bunch of introductory remarks, Saul addressed the congregation by telling a story.

A psychology student is invited to tour a psychiatric facility. As he walks through a common room, the fellow overhears patients talking with each other.

"Five!" One resident yells.

Another says, "thirty-three!"

After each number is shouted, the residents laugh and chuckle.

The visitor asks, "Is this a symptom of some ailment?"

"No," the guide replies. "These people have been here so long that rather than repeat the entire joke, they just number the jokes."

"Wow, that is clever."

After a moment, the visitor yells out, "fifteen!"

Nobody laughs.

"What happened?" he asks the guide.

"Well, you have to know how to tell a joke."

Saul paused.

"What do you think about my story?" he asked the audience.

Some members said the joke was funny; others wondered why he told it.

"Sometimes," Saul explained, "we use humor to entertain. Lots of times we use it to keep others at an emotional distance. For example, we might say something harsh and then claim to have just been kidding. That way, we get to speak our heartfelt feelings without taking responsibility for opening up and conversing with that person."

He paused.

"Let me ask you another question. What happens on an elevator?"

"You go up and down," an audience member exclaimed.

"You get to higher and lower floors fast without exerting much energy," another participant jested.

"Certainly, true statements. But, how do people react to each other?"

"You keep your personal distance – no eye contact, no touching," an elderly lady noted.

"Yes," the Leader continued. "When my neighbor steps outside on the way to her car, she typically says, 'How are you?' I understand the exchange is simply an acknowledgement of my presence. How inappropriate if I harangued her with a description of my most recent trauma. Likewise, how intrusive if I acted overly friendly toward strangers on an elevator."

After a brief pause, Saul continued.

"When close friends insist on talking solely about sports, movies, and the weather; when families insist on avoiding personal issues that might pack an emotional punch; when we are unwilling to express our intimate selves by substituting humor for feelings, we remain remote. It's like we're talking with the neighbor on her way to work. We avoid genuine relationships. If ethics is all about how we relate with others, we can't become ethical by avoiding relationships."

Again, he paused while we considered what he said.

"We bring meaning to our lives when we attempt to relate by inquiring about each other; by sharing joys, heartaches, fears, and accomplishments. Taking chances by opening to others is a form of intimacy. Otherwise, we are just throwing numbers at each other like the inmates of that psychiatric institute."

Another pause.

"And, being real with each other is lots cheaper than therapy."

On the way out, I chatted a bit with Doris. After all, she was now a friend.

ROAD RAGE

The driver in front of me was having a tough time deciding whether to go straight or turn left. The guy froze while the light changed from green to yellow before he turned at the last possible second to leave me in the red.

I honked loudly even as the offending motorist skedaddled.

I am retired and running an errand at the local grocery store to buy some vanilla soy milk along with cookies and a bunch of vitamin water drinks, perhaps some laundry detergent if it is on sale. Time is one of my luxuries.

When I'm occasionally confused about driving directions, I think the other drivers should just hold their horses. Have a little understanding for crying-out-loud. The world won't end because you had to wait a bit during my muddled moment.

Honking hardly lowered my stress. I bet it made the other driver irritated and anxious.

Then, I recalled how tolerance toward others brought out my best, how being overly critical dominated my childhood, and how I was responsible for my own decisions and happiness. Rather than cede power to the stranger, I thought about imagining if I was the momentarily confused driver. I suddenly felt better about both of us.

Madeline

CHAPTER 1

"Would you believe it, he can still perform?"

"Gwanma, you'w kidding," I heard Mom answer her mother.

"He was out of breath at the end. Exhausted. I had to push him off. What the hell. At seventy-five, he was ok."

I listened while folding clothes on the kitchen table. My little sister Camilla and I had just returned this Saturday morning from the laundromat after feeding coins into monstrous machines.

"Have you met anyone, Nadine?" Grandma asked.

"Nobody new," Mom replied. "Wou is awhays good fow some dough."

"Lou? He's such a big lug. How do you stand him?"

"He's wewhiabuh. And I onwy put out once in a whiwe. Pwhus, I'm no spwing chicken."

Mom told me that men come in two flavors, rats and suckers. Rats are lots of fun but end up dumping you. Suckers are weak. I was the product of a fling with a rat in the guise of a luggage salesman. Mom couldn't recall his name: "Your father left me with a couple of suitcases and you."

I kind of resemble her. At thirteen, I have her brown hair and round face. I'm on the shorter side and a bit pudgier than most of the girls in my class. I just started developing a figure with breasts and hips. My nose is not as flat as hers. Fortunately, I did not inherit her speech defect.

Camilla is Joe's daughter. She is three years younger than me and on the skinny side. According to Mom, Joe's a sucker.

"I don't know why I mawied that guy," Mom grumbled whenever Joe's name was mentioned. "But I know why I divowced him. A bookkeepah."

Not much money in that. I may be getting a bit fwuffy, but at wheast my idea of fun isn't doing cwoss wowd puzwhews."

Relationships with real men don't last, Mom maintained. She explained how they come into your life; then slip through your fingers like loose change.

"If you want to keep a wat, make the guy wait fow it," she would advise me. "I could nevwah do that. So, I'm stuck with you."

"Nadine, I need to stay with you for a few days," Grandma casually mentioned. "The old peoples' home is upset with me."

"No pwobhem. You can shweep in Maddy's bed fow a foow days."

I was already doing housework, meals, and laundry. Now, I would have to give up my bed and crawl in with Camilla.

"Nadine, I don't want my bed wet."

"Shut up. Gwanma can heaw you."

"I don't care."

"I wowk all day. I need my west. I'll give Gwammy a wubbuh sheet."

"You sleep with everyone, you sleep with her," I mumbled sarcastically.

"Don't wike it, get out," Nadine snarled.

My fun-loving mother worked as a sales clerk during the day. But, she liked to go out whenever a guy asked. Even when I was a child, she had me call her Nadine so that men might assume she wasn't my mother.

Living in a run-down duplex near Newark's Weequahic Park was dangerous.

I flashed back to the rough guy who grabbed me from behind in the park last week. When I turned and faced him, he told me I was cute. Even though he smelled awful, I asked if he would let me go if I kissed him. He laughed.

I kissed his cheek and broke free. Camilla could never do that.

"How about if I ask Joe to pick us up Saturday and keep us all weekend?" Nadine quickly nodded her assent.

Joe would come every Sunday to take Camilla and me someplace. Often it was only to get an ice cream cone and play at a local park. He cared. I wasn't his natural child. When he married Nadine, they had Camilla and Joe adopted me. I loved him for that. Even though Nadine was nominally Jewish, I loved having his exotic last name – Madallena. My name is Madeline Madallena. Nadine calls him mean names and gladly takes his weekly support payments

"Then Gwammy can have youw bed without you bewhy aching."

I didn't respond. I kept folding the laundry.

Am I real?

CHAPTER 2

"Hi, sweetie pie."

"Hey, Uncle Bill," I exclaimed.

"I was just in the neighborhood," he fibbed.

I knew Uncle Bill had to take a train and a bus to get from New York City to our home. Something was up.

"Oh, it's so good to see you," he said. "Look, I brought some rugelach and rye bread. Manhattan is the only place to find a decent bakery. Here's some delicatessen mustard, not that wimpy stuff. Turkey, cheese, and ham for sandwiches. Don't tell your mom. How about it?"

Everyone loves Uncle Bill. He's Nadine's brother. Bill lives in Manhattan by himself on the Lower East Side. He gets close to one-hundred percent disability from the army. And, he makes side money as a bridge partner playing with older ladies who just adore him. He also occupies himself by quilting pieces of fabric he retrieves from second-hand stores. Oh yeah, he loves visiting friends and relatives. And with just a bit of encouragement, he will dance gracefully despite having a roly-poly figure.

I bet you are wondering how he got disabled.

William was the youngest and only boy in a family of five. They coddled him. He loved being around the girls. He was totally gay, except nobody spoke about his peculiarity. When World War II broke out, Uncle Bill was drafted. He tried to tell the army recruiters about his preference, but they thought he was faking. Once drafted, he lasted about a week before becoming catatonic. After a year of psychiatric treatment at a veteran's hospital, the army honorably discharged Uncle Bill. He likes to tell us that he really fooled Uncle Sam.

"They thought I was totally nuts. They let me go with a nice monthly check. I tricked them," he bragged.

"Yeah," I said under my breath, "if being nuts for the rest of your life is tricking the army."

After I made sandwiches, we sat around the kitchen table.

"I talked with my dear sister last night. She is so upset with you Maddy. You two need to get away from each other."

"Any ideas?" I asked.

"Run away," he said.

"That's so crazy. Where would I go? I'm a kid, remember?"

"Joe. He remarried. He has a nice house with his new wife and her two daughters. What's a few more girls? Plus, if you demand to live with him, Joe stops paying child support. You and Camilla just pack your stuff and leave. Here, I have a bus schedule, sweetie."

Hmm, I thought. That old coot is not so off his rocker as he lets on.

CHAPTER 3

"What is it that you want, Maddy?" Samar asked.

"Well, I'm afraid, afraid to be disappointed. And, who says I deserve anything? Sometimes, I feel so unreal. It's almost like I am not here."

"First comes the anger," Susan declared. "That is how I know something is wrong. I learned that by paying attention to when I become too angry over too little, I could tell my early warning system is working. Then, I can try to figure out what is bothering me. It often helps when I talk it out with someone else."

"All I know is that when I feel bad about myself," Jeff added, "I start to get arrogant, so people will pull away. That way, it is their fault. Truth is, I sometimes feel underserving too. When I am down on myself, I wonder who would want anything to do with me?"

"How about if you don't know what is getting you upset or making you feel worthless?" I asked.

"Getting unstuck often begins with acknowledging that something ain't right," Tiana confessed. "When the pit of my stomach feels distressed, I need to pay attention. Kind of what Susan said."

Gary asked, "Maddy, how come you haven't answered Samar? What do you want?"

"I want to be treated as a person with substance. I want to feel like somebody," I responded.

"I can only speak for myself," Doris said. "I came to this group with pretty low self-esteem. You all helped me feel like I am important. You listen to me. Most importantly, I offer advice that seems helpful, at least to some of you. I feel needed. I feel liked."

"Nobody can make you feel like you are worthwhile," Gary said. "All we can do is let you know we admire your grit. Leaving home with your sister and all. How you feel about yourself needs to come from within, Maddy."

Joining this Ethical Group was the best thing since leaving Mom's place, I thought.

"My guess is that I need to face two demons," I quietly said.

"What do you mean?" Samar asked.

"First, I need to let Mom know that I forgive her. It takes way too much energy to stay resentful."

"What else?" Doris asked.

"I want some real friends. Perhaps, I could start with all of you. How about it?" I asked hopefully.

Marv Friedlander

Book 3

Some reflections are essays that convey a sense of humor about our human circumstances. Other essays offer a glimpse into what might be taken as insights into humanist values.

Reflections

PREVARICATE / PRI-ˈVER-ə-ˌKĀT: DEVIATE FROM THE TRUTH

have been thinking about public liars. That is, people in the public eye who brazenly falsify through 1) outright deception, 2) misleading statements, or 3) omission of crucial information.

The best in the business was Bill Clinton. He had the ability to look you in the eye through a camera lens and deliver sincerity with that slight rasp and Arkansas lilt. "I did not have sex with that woman!"

In this declaration, Bill hit the trifecta because he out-and-out lied about fooling around with a White House intern, misled by carefully crafting a statement that did not define the term "sex," and failed to inform us about his ribald shenanigans.

We have witnessed other notable prevaricators in all sorts of fields from Lance Armstrong (doping), to Pete Rose (gambling), to Gary Hart (Monkey Business), to Richard Nixon ("I am not a crook"), and the list goes on and on. We now have Trump and Roy Moore who believe that blustery denials and smearing accusers will save their political hides. People closest to them know the deceit. And, I believe the public knows deep down that they are colluding with liars by continuing to offer support. This is what is called the character issue. It should have been learned early in life.

We were at Grubers, a store located in downtown Irvington, New Jersey. Grubers specialized in clothing for boys and men. Mom took me to that store because it offered a selection of the euphemistically described "husky" sizes. I would try the pants on; the salesman would call the tailor to mark them with some sort of white chalk to shape the seat, shorten the length, and prepare the cuffs. As the salesman and Mom were chit-chatting, I wandered over to a display case full of shiny objects. I quickly spotted a bright, red, swiss army knife that soon ended up in my pocket.

A few days later, Mom asked how I had acquired the knife. Stupidly, I had secreted it in one of my drawers. How was I to know that as she put in freshly washed and folded socks, she would make her discovery? Kids are sometimes so dumb. I immediately folded.

"I took it from Grubers," I confessed.

"Wow," Mom gushed, "you were fast. However, we have to return it right now."

And, that is exactly what happened. I had to walk up to the salesman and tell him that I took the knife without having paid for it. He was more embarrassed than me. I immediately got it. He did not want to lose a good customer (three sons and a father).

"You are very brave young man. Thanks."

That was it. My conscience was clear. More importantly, I had been caught stealing and received a punishment early in my criminal career. I suspect that as a younger kid, I was taught about lying because I become overly heated and stumble and feel guilty and eventually "fess up" when I try to tell a whopper.

Perhaps had Bill, Lance, Pete, Gary, Richard, Roy, and Donald had similar experiences, they would have been willing to admit to indiscretions later in life. They might have taken their punishment, cleared their consciences, and become persons with integrity.

LET'S PLAY

We were experiencing the first autumn at our new home. I eagerly began raking the incredible number of leaves that had already dropped from the large maple and oak trees that dotted our large corner property.

As I rested on my rake and admired my leaf mound before stuffing the pile into bags, I recalled that as a kid the reward for having piled leaves into the gutter was setting a blazing fire. Now, my satisfaction would come from having sweated a bit, enjoyed the crisp air against my face, delighted in smelling the earthy odor of autumn leaves, and appreciated a cleared lawn.

While I dreamily relaxed, I noticed Sarah and Joseph from my corner vision. Immediately, I foresaw the logical consequence of a pile of leaves and two little kids. This would be my moment of truth.

They leaped, rolled, laughed, and knocked my work about. Some twenty years later, I still enjoy the smell of fallen leaves, the feel of crisp air against my face, and a cleaned lawn. However, I miss the fun of watching my kids jump into a pile of carefully gathered leaves.

THE KUNG FU KID

Toward the end of each academic year, Mrs. White produced a children's talent show for the elementary school my kids attended. This bigger-than-life teacher encouraged our students to participate. She also emceed the show. Kids loved this chance to demonstrate their talents and observe their peers perform. Parents beamed believing their child was a potential star.

Held in an all-purpose room, magicians, singers, pianists, dancers, accordionists, and comedians walked on stage to perform for teachers, students, and parents. It's been over twenty years. However, I still recall two performances.

A youngster dressed in a white karate gi appeared on stage. Mrs. White told us that he would be breaking a board with his bare hands. The kid looked little, the board looked thick, and the older brother holding the board looked doubtful.

"Please, we need silence. Guy must concentrate."

Whack! Guy struck the board and winced. Before hitting the board again, Guy appeared hesitant. Whack! I could see tears welling as he grabbed his striking hand in obvious pain. While he paused to gather his courage, Mrs. White walked swiftly to Guy and put her arm around him.

"This is a lot harder than it appears. Guy broke a board in practice. Let's give him a big hand."

We applauded. As Guy left the stage with his head low, his parents took over from Mrs. White.

Then a young girl appeared on stage in a kind of cowgirl outfit. Laura belted out a popular country song and brought the house down. I was excited for her moxie and thrilled for her parents. Yet, I wondered how Guy might remember this afternoon.

The best and worst of times, that is how I believe we experience our school days. We totter between exhilaration one moment and despair the next. Nevertheless, it is often an adult's steady hand and encouraging words that makes all the difference.

CONSCIENCE

Jack and I tumbled after each other through the living room where we broke a vase, past the kitchen where we destroyed a chair, and into the bathroom where we landed with a thud against the sink. One minute the sink was fine; the next it was detached with water spurting from suddenly disconnected pipes.

My brother and I immediately stopped roughhousing. I could see his horrified look, a look that he likely saw on my face. Our parents would not be returning from their evening out for a while. But, the emergency filling the bathroom floor was happening now.

"What are we going to do?" Jack asked.

"Don't know. Wait, let's get Mr. Osterweill."

Mr. Osterweill lived next door. He was the long-suffering neighbor who never yelled at us despite the outdoor lights that illuminated our make-shift basketball court and shown directly into his den. We never heard a peep from him despite our basketball continuously rolling into his bushes. We were never chastised despite the noise we made playing evening pickup games.

"Mr. Osterweill, we need help. Jack and I broke the sink and Mom and Dad are out and . . ."

"Hold your horses. Let me get some shoes on. I'll meet you at your house."

Meanwhile, Jack had gotten every towel he could find and began dam construction. Then, Mr. Osterweill walked in.

"Come on, Marv. Let me show you something."

I followed him to our basement.

"This is your main shut-off water supply valve."

He turned the valve.

"Let's see about the damage," he suggested.

We returned to the bathroom. Sure enough, the water had stopped.

"OK," he said. "Mop it up and good luck boys."

Mom and Dad had seen a movie. Before returning home, they had stopped to purchase some bakery goods to enjoy with coffee. They were in a good mood when they walked in.

That did not last long.

They were not overly upset with the destruction our mayhem had caused until Mom noticed the broken vase. Sentimental value was not a concept I would understand for many years. I made an insincere apology. However, I was beginning to understand that my actions had consequences.

The next evening, I kept our basketball lights off. I would not turn them on again.

"I'LL HAVE A NUMBER THREE, PLEASE"

One evening, I was waiting in line at a Popeyes Louisiana Kitchen fast food restaurant in New Orleans. I know, sacrilege. But, I was tired, it was late, and I just wanted to take out something to eat before returning to my hotel room.

Suddenly, a hefty employee lifted herself over the counter and ran past the customers.

"Rats! Dear God, I seen a rat!"

Customers scattered. Employees dashed about frantically. Finally, a manager said that he killed the rat.

"Crushed that sucker with a mop."

On my way out, I observed that most of the customers quietly reformed their lines. I thought about docile people who accept their circumstances.

While it is true that Popeyes, like other fast-food places, serves carefully measured and heavily salted fried and grilled food with lots of paper and plastic, it is us docile customers who have little regard for our dignity and bodies that most bothers me. When we don't value ourselves, how are we going to care about others?

For now, I am resisting becoming acculturated to being so easily exploited. I gave up fast food that evening.

GRANDMA

The gist of the argument is that we hold dearly to beliefs developed early in life because of sociological and physiological factors. Despite counterfactual information, we stubbornly cling to ideas absorbed from those with whom we spend our formative years – this is the sociological factor. Early ideas are also imprinted in the reptilian part of our brain – the physiological factor.

Accordingly, we're going to continue to believe what we believed as exemplified by the following story.

My father was raised by his mother in the Bronx because his parents separated over irreconcilable differences: Both were stubborn and uncommunicative. Grandpa Joe earned a living with his brother by operating a used furniture store. He was the mostly silent muscle who hauled furniture around the store and to and from customers. Grandma Fanny had operated a beauty salon from her home. She was a petite, carefully groomed, grey-haired lady who now lived off social security and Dad's monthly contribution. She did not like to travel, and she disliked people.

One day, I was dropped off at my grandmother's Bronx apartment. At the age of six, this would be the first and only time we would meet. Her apartment was a fourth-floor walk-up. The place was meticulous. Every bit of ancient furniture, every doily-topped table, every old-fashioned lamp was without a speck of dust. On a coffee table, she had prepared a bit of candy for her visiting grandchild.

"They look like pebbles," I said.

"Try one," Fanny answered.

"Will they break my teeth?"

"Eat it or not."

I bravely plopped a speckled rock into my mouth. At first, it refused to crack. Then, miraculously, it split into a chocolate treat. I smiled. She cracked the briefest of grins.

"Come on, Marvin. We're going out."

She took me to places she knew.

First, we walked to a corner grocery store where she bought me a small bottle of Coca-Cola. Then, we walked to a subway station. I had never been on the New York subway.

After Fanny inserted tokens into a turnstile, we entered past barred gates. The place was kind of dingy with pieces of paper lazily tossing about from breezes that flowed around the platform. A rusting vending machine sat in the twilight offering packets of Dentyne. A sharp rasp and loud squeal followed by a roar and stiff wind announced our train's arrival. Fanny grabbed my hand and led me into a car. We whirred past dimly lit tiled walls. As the train rushed from station to station, street names would suddenly appear on walls illuminated by a single light. We got off at a station that looked exactly like the one we had entered. After climbing a grimy staircase, we were someplace else.

We walked a few blocks to a small park where she sat us on a bench.

"Now we talk, Marvin," she proclaimed.

Her idea of talking was to tell me that she did not think her son would amount to much because he had been a sickly youngster. She would have nothing to do with my Grandpa Joe. My mother was way too bossy. We lived too far away in New Jersey for her to visit. And, I was to avoid bats.

"Bats are dangerous. They fly silently from rooftops at your head. You can't see or hear them. Once they get into your hair, they can't escape. Then, they will bite your scalp."

With that, she was finished.

We walked a bit around the park. Then, we returned on the subway to her shoddy but clean apartment where we silently awaited my departure.

When Dad came to pick me up, he did not hug or kiss his mother. He simply knocked at the door and left with me. But, I asked Grandma Fanny for something before I left. I asked to take a few pieces of her rock candy.

"Sure, I can't eat it," she said.

I did not eat it either. I saved the pieces for many years. And yes, I firmly believe that we are best off by avoiding bats because they are likely to become entrapped in our hair.

FUN WITH DICK

Johnny Carson was interviewing Dick Clark on the "Tonight Show." Dick was touting yet another rock & roll television special. Surprisingly, the usually lightweight interviewer asked Clark a serious question.

"Dick, you have been covering rock music from the beginning. What does it all mean?"

"What are you asking, Johnny?" Dick responded.

"Well, you got your big break in Philadelphia in the late 1950s with American Bandstand. You have been associated with rock music for some forty years. I was wondering whether you developed some ideas about its significance."

Dead air on television is lethal. Silence emanated from a flustered Dick Clark caught off guard by a serious inquiry. Perhaps Carson had only one intellectual question in him. This was it. Finally, after what seemed an interminable pause, Dick responded.

"I'm not sure, Johnny. I never thought about it."

"And now a word from our sponsor. . . ."

I don't think I'm arguing against devouring our fair share of pop culture. I think I'm suggesting that some amount of analysis of what we are reading and viewing and hearing – our own analysis, right or wrong, cockeyed or insightful – is what a curious person does. Otherwise, we are merely passive vessels who absorb and reflect the daily pabulum.

TALES OF THE SUPERMARKET

"Where's the duck sauce?" a customer asked me.

"Well, I'm not sure. Let me find out."

Why would a customer at Wegmans, an upscale supermarket, come to the pizza station to ask about duck sauce for his food bar meal? No matter, we were instructed to make sure customers receive top notch treatment. I figured I would ask one of the people assigned to schlepp food from the kitchen to the food bars. No dice. Then, I thought that one of my pizza colleagues would know for sure.

"Frank, where's the duck sauce?"

"What's that?" Frank responded.

"I thought you were Chinese. Don't you guys eat duck sauce with your egg rolls?"

Frank rolled his eyes and said something guttural in his native tongue. Frank was his Wegmans' name. His real first name was Huizhang.

Eventually, I found the plastic packets near the checkout line nestled in a basket alongside miniature size portions of mustard, ketchup, mayonnaise, salt, and pepper. By the time I returned with packets for the customer, he was gone.

I never found out whether Frank was pulling my leg about the duck sauce. He was a hardworking man of few words. He looked out for me by refusing to let the old guy perform heavy lifting or clean the deep fryer.

"Baba, you take care of the customer. I'll take care of the fryer."

For two years, I worked closely with Frank. He worked evening shifts as a second job. Toward the end of our shift one day, Frank approached me.

"I will not be working here after tonight, Baba."

"How come?" I asked.

"I finally got a position with George Mason University."

"Oh, that's good. What are you going to be doing?"

"I will be an assistant professor in the Department of Computer Science."

I was dumbfounded. This hardworking, self-effacing guy had emigrated to the United States with an advanced degree in computer science from China. He spent several years learning English. He took a day job doing computer technical support. And, he worked during the evenings making pizza. I also learned that he had a wife and a daughter.

After we finished cleaning the pizza station for the evening, I shook his hand.

I thanked Huizhang for being so generous toward me. And, I gave him a couple of packets of duck sauce.

OUR FAMILY MOVED, A LOT

As Dad's business ventures succeeded, we moved from Newark's inner city toward the outer suburbs; from modest homes to more elegant dwellings. Each move required acclimation to a new school. Because Dad and Mom were busy operating their beauty salon business, they adopted a self-reliant philosophy for their children. Self-reliance meant that we were told the names and proximate direction of our new schools.

I once counted eleven moves through my high school years.

Mt. Vernon Elementary School was located about a mile from our new house on the outskirts of Newark, New Jersey.

"Off you go, Marvin. Stick to the main streets. Your school is in the shadow of the Ivy Hill Park Apartments. Here's your lunch."

"What's the name, again?" I asked.

"Mt. Vernon. Just ask someone if you get lost," Mom advised.

About ten in the morning, I began to get tired of walking in what seemed like my own footsteps. Desperate and a bit hungry, I began asking. However, people were in a hurry. Plus, stores did not want kids loitering. I finally stopped at a building that was not a store. It was a synagogue.

After I walked in, I found a classroom. I knew this was not my grammar school, but I sat at a desk and began to eat lunch. An older man approached. We talked for a while. I explained my predicament. He laughed and said that he knew how to get to my school.

"Sometimes the lost lamb stumbles into a rich pasture."

The rabbi talked in parables. When I took Hebrew lessons from Rabbi Jacob Mendelsohn, he would remind me of our accidental meeting.

"I told you. If God wishes, you will find your way back."

Over the years, I abandoned the religious fervor that drove me toward Judaism. But, I never abandoned my appreciation for the kindness extended to some little kid the Reb found enjoying an early lunch in his synagogue.

HUMILITY

"That is amazing!" I sputtered.

Joseph and I were out for one of our early evening walks around the neighborhood. We had just passed a middle-aged lady walking a small dog on a leash with one hand. With her other hand, she pushed a bright pink stroller. We were both expecting a little baby under the hood. Instead, the stroller held a small white dog.

"Now, I have seen just about everything," I told him.

Joseph is incredibly tolerant and agreeable. Unwilling to say a bad word about another person, he merely nodded.

"She is treating a dog like a baby," I exclaimed.

As we passed another walker, I asked what she thought about the lady with the baby stroller and the dogs.

"I see her walking her dogs like that all the time. It is unusual."

Yesterday, I was watering newly planted grass seed in the front of our house when the stroller-lady appeared walking toward me. I wanted to hear her voice and confirm my suspicion that this was one crazy lady.

"Hi, is that a Maltese?"

"No, the one on the leash is a Westie."

"And the one in the stroller?"

"Oh, that is a tiny Maltese. She is a rescue dog. I took her in because, unfortunate thing, she can't walk very well. But, she just loves going out to get some fresh air."

"Wow. That is awfully kind of you," I declared.

"My only regret is that the stroller is so pink. Someone gave it to me to help with the little one."

THANKSGIVING

Mom was an excellent short order cook. She could whip up ham and Velveeta cheese baked into a crescent roll in a flash, scramble eggs with onions and tomatoes in a blink, and efficiently broil a steak with a heaping mess of mashed potatoes. Her mother had died when Mom was a child; so, her quick cooking skills developed as a necessity while she cared for her father and two younger brothers during the Great Depression.

Then, one Thanksgiving when our relatives were due to arrive later that day, our maid called out sick. What to do? What to do?

"Marv, do you know how to cook a turkey?" Mom asked.

Brief confession. All my life, I have been unwilling to disappoint others. Can I cook a turkey?

"Sure. Nothing to it."

"Ok, I will make mashed potatoes, yams, string beans, salad, cranberry sauce, and packaged stuffing. I will also put the rolls into the oven. You do the turkey."

There it was. A giant bird, a giant bird tightly bound inside a white plastic wrapping. I first looked at the wrapper hoping it would offer cooking instructions. Alas, the covering provided information about the bird's weight, water content, and added ingredients. Nothing about preparing the critter for our large family and guests.

"Marv, you OK? Need any help?"

"Nope. Just fine."

After another moment or two of panic, I reached back into my recollection. No help from my reading Davy Crockett or the Black Stallion. Then, I recalled something from the family television shows I liked.

"Remove the gizzards and place the bird into a bag to retain its moisture."

I think that advice was from "Father Knows Best." But, it might have been "The Adventures of Ozzie and Harriet." Or, maybe it was from "What's My Line?"

I dutifully cut open the plastic liner and lifted the bird with both hands into a large pan. Then, I looked in the cabinet under the sink where we kept our brown supermarket bags opposite the cleansers.

I began to whistle a happy tune.

After sliding the bird into the bag, all that was left was to turn on the oven and set the timer. Easy peasy.

"Mom, if you were cooking a big chicken what temperature would you set the oven?"

"Oh, I never cook chicken in the oven. I once made chicken cacciatore in a frying pan. You take a cut up chicken, add a can of spaghetti sauce . . . ."

"Never mind."

I decided that 375 degrees would work because it was higher than 300 and less than 400. And, I decided that taking the bird out an hour before mealtime would also work because that would give us time to get it ready with the other stuff. After placing the pan with the turkey stuffed inside a brown paper bag into the oven, I decided to go outside for a while to calm down.

Guests, greetings, fuss and bother. Everyone was hungry. Mom and I had the table set. True to her word, she had prepared bowl after bowl of accompaniments. I asked for her help in taking the hot pan from the oven. At eleven, you are just not that strong. The bag was a greasy mess. After I carefully de-stuck the bag from a couple of places on the bird's skin, the turkey looked and smelled fantastic.

"Wow!" I exhaled.

"Excellent Marvin. You did know how to cook that turkey after all."

"DUNKIRK"

Friends recommended this movie for its showing the "terror and bravery of the English in their Darkest Hour." They also raved about realistic air battles. A few people disliked the music – too loud; the continuity – too confusing; the Germans – too few; the dialogue – too hard to understand; the importance of the battle – too unexplained; and the accuracy – too wrong. One person declared, "It's simply events strung together." Critics seemed unanimous in praising this movie for its excitement and realism. Well!

The movie often had me on the edge of my seat. Compelling editing focused my attention (Hill Street Blues I think was the first time I recall the magic where several related stories are told through fast-paced vignettes) from air to sea to land. This flick made the heroics and cowardice and indifferent luck (or lack thereof) immediate by concentrating on a few individual stories. How is that we know the war's ultimate outcome (Allies win), yet remain fascinated by a rousing telling of a strategic retreat by the British against overwhelming German forces.

I thought the music was spot on because it helped maintain tension when survival - of individuals and whole platoons – is at stake. As with the PBS showing of English drawing room and mystery television shows, I would have enjoyed subtitles. "Britain and America are two nations divided by a common language." I would rather have a compelling movie that is a bit inaccurate than a bland docudrama (see, Shakespeare's history plays). I especially appreciated the panoply of experiences of men under stress without judgement – the brave, the shell-shocked, the exhausted, and the survivalists. Is a soldier whose forces have been decimated where retreat is the order of the day a coward for trying to escape at any cost?

On senior discount Wednesdays, the crowd is older. I was sorry that I did not ask some in the audience whether they recalled Dunkirk. After seeing this show, I certainly will never forget it.

THE PRICE

Sarah and I were on our way to New York City. I had arranged for us to stay in a rooming-style place on the upper east side. The room would cost a lot less than the $400 per-night price tag for a real hotel room for two adults with separate beds. We needed a place located near Manhattan Marymount College where my daughter would be auditioning for admittance to the school's dance program.

When we arrived, I paid the $30 per day parking fee at a nearby garage. We then got access to the room that had been advertised as having two sleeping spaces, a living room, and a kitchenette. The room was located on the first floor. It had the requisite iron bars across the windows. The miniature living space came complete with a fold-out couch, one chair, and a counter with a microwave. It also had a tiny bathroom with a toilet and shower. Up a short staircase, the second-floor area was completely covered in mirrors – I'm talking walls and ceiling here. The floor was covered with a mattress that took up the entire space. Sarah said she would sleep in the "loft" because it would be easier for her to crouch beneath the low ceiling.

Turns out that applicants for entrance to a college dance program must pass the usual academic requirement plus be approved through an audition. I had lots of fun taking Sarah to various schools. Some permitted me to watch the rehearsals. Other schools ushered its helicopter parents far away from the action.

Turns out that after Sarah auditioned at Marymount, she was confident that her dancing would get her admitted. I was not so sure about the school's tuition and housing costs. But, we had several colleges in our basket and we would decide after lots of talking and number crunching.

The head of the dance department informed us on the spot about who would be accepted and who did not make the cut. Sarah did not make the cut. We were shocked because everybody accepted was a person of color.

On the drive home, Sarah and I joked about the "fancy" hotel room. We did not joke so much about the audition result.

"Are you angry, upset, annoyed?" I asked. "It was not right, what happened at that audition."

"I'm disappointed. I thought I had danced well. I was definitely superior to the other girls," Sarah replied.

"Well, what do you think happened?"

"I think I am paying the price for years of discrimination. I think I will find a college dance program that is just fine for me."

And, that is exactly what happened.

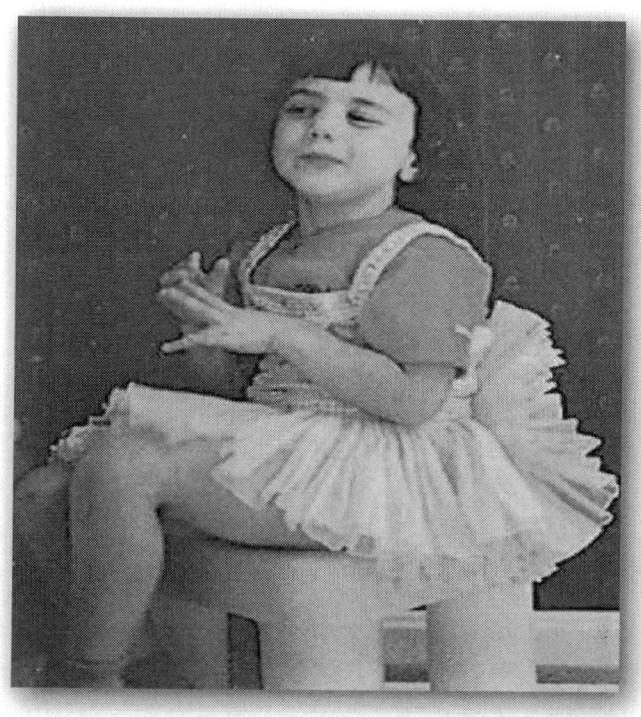

LET THEM EAT CAKE

Like Johnny Cash, Dad dressed for work in black. His dashing, debonair, mysterious, and dangerous attire suited the assumed persona of Mr. André - haute coiffure. I did not know until years later that certain jobs came with stereotypes.

Teaching was a feminine occupation; whereas, accounting was male. Beauticians were women unless they were gay men. As portrayed by "The Man In The Grey Flannel Suit," life in the 1950s offered safety to those who obeyed cultural norms and havoc for nonconformists. If you lived outside society's strict lines, you were fair game for insult, discrimination, and worse.

We had names for gay people.

I recall reading "The Ballad of Reading Gaol" in which Oscar Wilde lamented that prison was the penalty for love outside the lines.

> A prison wall was round us both,
> Two outcast men were we:
> The world had thrust us from its heart,
> And God from out His care:
> And the iron gin that waits for Sin
> Had caught us in its snare.

And now, despite noble words about tolerance, human and civil rights, and equal protection under the law, some people are refused the right to order a wedding cake at a bakery.

"No cake for you!"

I suppose this type of affront might seem relatively mild. Some might suggest that a gay person should just suck it up if a bakery refuses to make a cake to help celebrate a marriage, a baby adoption or an anniversary. Just buy a supermarket cake to grieve the loss of a partner. I am sure the sting of rejection will fade.

I now get why Dad wore black. It was dangerous to be considered gay. Unfortunately, I don't think that wearing black will help with ordering a wedding cake from a religious bigot.

WILD HORSEMAN

Helene had an abbreviated career as a piano prodigy. Abbreviated because she spent what should have been her career years consigned to a Nazi concentration camp. After immigrating to America, Helene Newman offered piano lessons to America's kinder.

Mary and I were like the rest of our family . . . musically appreciative but tunefully dense. We hear the difference between a C or an F, a sharp or a flat, and whether someone has a good singing voice. We simply cannot carry a tune in a bucket. Nevertheless, Mom had acquired a beautiful piano for which she had her heart set on appreciating her two eldest perform to the delight of her friends.

Bearing dark blue numbers tattooed on her forearm, this dignified woman - despite past indignities - agreed to teach piano to us. We dutifully slogged through John Thompson books, practiced our scales, and tried to learn music theory. Toward the end of each lesson when Ms. Newman stopped my struggles a bit early, we had a moment to talk. I think we were both relieved.

"Ms. Newman, what was it like?"

"What do you mean, Marvin?"

"The war, the camp, your life?"

"Nobody who did not endure the fear, the deprivations, the loss of everything can appreciate what happened."

"How did you survive?"

"People will do anything to survive. You think to yourself, 'I would not do this or that.' Then, you are starving, cold, and fearful. You do it. And, you do worse."

"How did you get better?"

"I forgave myself, dear boy."

We never talked about how little talent I demonstrated.

The farthest I achieved was Robert Schumann's Op. 68, No. 8 (The Wild Horseman). Looking back, I think Ms. Newman could not bear to listen to my rendition of other classics. So, the lessons ended with that piece.

When I despair about the degradation of our democracy and civility, I appreciate that people survived worse than this. Eventually, the light returns.

And, thankfully, others are capable of perfect harmony.

COMFORT FOOD

Because my parents worked at their small business six days a week, they rarely relaxed with their five children. But, Sunday brunch around our breakfast nook was devoted to the family when we talked politics, books, theater, and world affairs while munching our way through comfort food.

Dad would leave early in the morning to gather salt sticks, bagels, rye bread, cream cheese, nova lox, white fish, and schmaltz herring. Mom would put up the coffee, which we consumed under her watchful eye by making half and half (milk and coffee). She also prepared a fancy plate of lettuce, tomato, Bermuda onions, and pickled beets.

At first, we children were relegated to listening to the conversation. When they considered us sufficiently mature, we were individually invited to join the discussion. First, they invited my older sister. Then my turn began when Mom asked, "Marvin, what do you think about government subsidies for private schools?"

I wonder whether they were interested in my opinion, trying to pros-elytize, or teaching me how to argue. Perhaps, it was all three because when I expressed my opinion - an opinion made up on the spot - that private school students were as deserving as those who attended a public institu-tion, my parents exploded in vehement disagreement.

"Don't you know that public education takes care of everyone without excluding the disabled, the underachiever, or the poor?"

"Well," I answered, "my experience demonstrates that public schools teach to the mediocre. High achievers and low achievers are not properly served. The disabled are given shoddy treatment. Why shouldn't the gov-ernment support educational programs for kids who don't fit the norm?"

"If we fully support public education, government serves everyone."

"That is not what occurs," I suggested. "Why not make it possible through government funds to provide more middle and lower income stu-dents the opportunity for a private education?"

"Why should the government support parochial education?"

Back and forth we argued. I learned to appreciate the fun of the argument.

What I find most discouraging is that we now refuse to give each other the benefit of arguing from different perspectives. We make it personal. We are intolerant. We often refuse to permit the other person to finish. We ascribe evil to the person rather than disagreement with the position. Win or die.

Perhaps it was the food and pleasure of family time before the beginning of another week, perhaps it was because we liked and respected each other, perhaps it was because we understood that by listening to each other we might learn something. Nevertheless, our Sunday brunches ended in good humor.

"Pass the lox, please."

TURKEY

Today's meal will feature turkey, boxed stuffing, instant mashed potatoes, and canned yams with the marshmallow topping. We will also serve a side of cranberry sauce – ridges showing. Plus, one of us will microwave some broccoli and cauliflower. A bagged romaine salad will round out the spread along with some ready-made biscuits. Fortunately, I purchased a "home-made" pumpkin pie from Wegmans (local, upscale supermarket).

I put my foot down about the string bean and mushroom soup casserole. You must draw the line between we ain't such great cooks and tacky and tasteless.

I recall dating a terrific cook. Terry offered to make Thanksgiving dinner at her home. My sister and her boyfriend drove from New York City to join us in Fairfax, Virginia. The food was terrific. Each dish was gourmet style with lots of ingredients. Suddenly, Rich turned red and started to choke.

"What's wrong, what's the matter?" I yelled.

"Rena asked, "What was in that stuffing?"

Terry explained that it was her family's heirloom recipe. Along with the usual bread crumbs, onions, garlic, celery, milk, butter and seasoning, the recipe called for diced oysters.

Rena rushed Rich to the emergency room to treat his shellfish allergy. He was given a shot of something or other to relieve his air passages. They did not return to finish their meal. I sort of blamed my girlfriend for almost killing the boyfriend.

A few years later, my sister would have been only too glad had the guy been fatally done in by the oyster stuffing.

So, I appreciate our run-of-the-mill Thanksgiving feast. I am content with eating ordinary food and appreciating having all of us together without any added drama.

ROCKY

I encountered Lee in my apartment complex gym. We chit-chatted while working out. He looked a bit odd until I realized that he simply held his head forward and kept his eyes and mouth open wide as if in perpetual anticipation. He was also going prematurely bald. Unfortunately, he styled his back hair forward.

I learned that he also liked jogging.

"Let's meet after work," I suggested. "We can run the trail behind our apartment building."

"OK," he agreed. "I'll call you when I get home from work tomorrow."

"Marv, I'm about ready. Come on down. I'll leave my apartment door unlocked."

When I arrived, Lee was ready.

"Let's go," I suggested.

"Wait. We need some inspiration."

It was in the next moment that I realized that we operated so differently."

"Huh?"

Lee flipped a switch on his music box. Out poured the Rocky theme evoking the image of that "ham and egger" who mastered the steps leading to the top of the Philadelphia Museum of Art. By the song's final crescendo, both Rocky and Lee were in comparable states of exhilaration.

"Lee, we are only going to jog for a few miles on the path behind our apartment building."

In addition to his somewhat goofy look, Lee told me that he was having trouble with the people at work and with getting dates. I offered some suggestions.

"Think about how you might want to be treated. Calm down a bit because people are put off by mistaking your enthusiasm for aggression."

"I always act like this. It is who I am."

"Perhaps you might look at yourself in the mirror. Practice holding your head a bit back. Think about how keeping your eyes so wide and mouth so open might make you seem goofy. You might also consider just cropping your hair."

"That is just who I am, Marv."

"Take clues from other people. If they are calm, you might want to slow down a bit. At work, ask how your colleagues might want to proceed. With a girl, look at her body language. Is she feeling overwhelmed."

"I can't change. More importantly, I don't want to change."

The next time I saw Lee at the gym, he told me that he had quit his job and was moving to Israel. He thought he might join a kibbutz.

"Why?"

"I might meet a girl. I have a friend who did that. People won't be so critical."

My friendship with Lee taught me a couple of important lessons.

I had been rude and arrogant to believe that I had the right to dictate what he needed and effectuate change. Being a sounding board? Yes. Feeding back what I heard? Certainly. Asking questions? Definitely. Telling someone who they are, how they might be defective, and how they might live? No.

Secondly, friendship requires reciprocity – a mutuality that includes enjoying the other person's companionship and affording respect.

I neither respected Lee nor enjoyed his company. I was a critic.

Whether he achieved his dream in Israel on a kibbutz with a girl, I never found out. He was certainly better off without my miserable friendship.

A GIRL'S VIEW

One day when Sarah was three years old and her grandmother was visiting from Saint Louis, Sarah noticed that "we are both wearing pink socks."

"We are twins," Grandma replied. "And we are both wearing sweaters."

Sarah though for a moment before asking, "Are you wearing underpants?"

"Yes," Grandma answered.

"We really are twins!" Sarah exclaimed.

I read in today's Washington Post that orthodox Judaism does not certify women as rabbis because of twelfth century religious writings that ascribe authoritative roles to men. It has something to do with Kosher butchers being men.

That some women are willing to accept second-class status does not justify such treatment for others. I recall reading that when the constitutional right for women to vote was being vigorously promoted, many women argued against what became the 19th Amendment. Rationalization that justifies discrimination based on gender, sexual identity, race, or age is just that - an excuse to justify bias.

Like Sarah trying to emulate her grandmother, we need strong role models to produce a vibrant society. It is important that we eliminate restrictions that hold back equal opportunity by striving to remove both blatant and subtle forms of discrimination.

Taxes

PART 1

Some say they don't understand how people can handle difficulty and tragedy in their lives without a belief in God.

Who is to deny someone reliance on God as being important to their coping with dire situations? Conversely, who is to deny anyone the right to rely on their own fortitude during times of crisis? There is no fixed rule about what we must believe to overcome hardship. As circumstances change, we are free to try different strategies.

Humanism advises tolerance for individual beliefs provided they do not impinge on the liberties of others.

I believe that being cared for by someone during a tough time can be as meaningful to the humanist as receiving a benediction that asks for God's blessing is to the believer. While we do not require another person's approval to follow our beliefs, a little empathy and respect works wonders.

PART 2

"Taxes are what we pay for a civilized society." These words by Oliver Wendell Holmes, Jr., made me feel good about my work after having been hired out of college by the Internal Revenue Service to conduct taxpayer examinations.

On this day, the price of a civilized society boiled down to a guy sitting across from me because someone selecting tax returns for examination did not believe that the man made so little income from hot dogs and soda sold at high school football games. The hot dog man was the subject of my audit.

I knew from personal experience that not all the hot dogs cooked on football game day are sold for their full price because my friend Jay and I would wait until late in the fourth quarter before making our move. Then, we would approach the vendor's aluminum cart with twelve-year-old swagger and offer five cents for a hot dog.

"Tell you what. Pay one dollar, take five hot dogs."

The bargaining went swiftly as the game clock ran down. We usually got the dogs we wanted for ten cents each with a roll and mustard and relish before the final horn sounded.

"No sauerkraut for that price!"

We passed up on drinks.

On the other hand, the guy sitting across the table owned a house in a suburban community. He had a job during the week and worked high school football games on weekends. I knew we were going to reach a deal. I just had to get there methodically. If I tried to cut to the chase by presenting him with an increased tax obligation, he would have been outraged. Something in us wants to feel like we are being treated fairly.

So, I started with the expense side of the ledger. Hot dogs and buns purchased less product spoilage. Then I figured out how many hot dogs with buns were likely sold to figure out gross profits. I also calculated an amount of food product the family devoured. Same with the sodas and other snacks sold to hungry fans.

In addition to my favorite Oliver Wendell Holmes, Jr., quote, I kept another inspirational statement handy that helped me rationalize my job:

"Civilization is but a thin veneer stretched across the passions of the human heart. And civilization doesn't just happen; we have to make it happen." Bill Moyers

The hot dog vender and I reached an agreement after I finagled some numbers to take ten percent off his tax bill.

Was I implementing the lofty principles of our American experiment by collecting tax revenues? Was I keeping the thin veneer of civilization intact by enforcing taxpayer honesty?

In looking back, I think I was just a young man with a government job trying to do my best. Any claim to lofty principles rested on a belief in fairness that also considered how another person might want to be treated. Ultimately, I discovered that I was applying an ethical approach to how we might treat each other at home, play, and work. Perhaps empathy for the other person and for ourselves is how we maintain civilization.

Plus, I had a fondness for a guy selling hot dogs from a cart at high school football games.

A Holiday Story

Mom decided we should get away to Florida during that endlessly drab winter because she was mad, again, at Dad.

After soaking up a week's worth of the semi-tropics at a Miami Beach hotel, we boarded a National Airlines prop for our return trip to Newark airport.

"Attention. Please fasten your seat belts. The captain has turned on the no smoking light. All trays and seats must be placed in their upright position."

The plane began to jerk upwards and down. Mom huddled a bit more tightly into her mink coat. Mary and Jack anxiously looked at each other. I regretted having eaten the sandwich and chips and peanuts.

"This is the captain. We are running into some weather. I will be taking the plane to a higher altitude. Just bear with us and remain in your seats, please."

As the plane rocked and tilted, swayed and dipped; as my stomach whooshed with each sudden descent; as my forehead broke into a cold sweat and my palms became sweaty, I heard Mom's voice.

"Children, I will never, ever again be too angry with your Dad."

As she made her promise – I suppose in exchange for keeping the plane from crashing – I vomited.

An amazing thing happened after I threw up. Like a domino effect, row upon row of scared travelers were now violently ill.

The stewardesses were too green to thank us for flying with National when we finally landed at La Guardia rather than at Newark Airport. The captain and co-pilot were off the plane as quickly as the ground crew released the cockpit door. We passengers straggled around the messes with our carry-on baggage, stuffed alligators, and heavy coats.

Miraculously, Dad was waiting for us as we limped, pallid and weak, from the gate's ramp into the airport arrival area.

"I drove from Newark through the storm when they announced the airport change," he told us.

"Oh, Wally."

Emily

Located on Leslie street in the heart of Newark's Clinton Hill neighborhood with its graceful elm trees and elegant houses, our Federalist-style home proudly showed its brick construction and slate roof. When we moved, the gas and electricity had not been turned on. The first neighbors to visit were four children and a mom from the clapboard house situated directly across the street. Herman, Irwin, Charlotte, and Phyllis were happy to have new friends in the neighborhood with whom our brood roughly matched.

Emily was the mom. Short, stout, and frizzy haired, she was never without an apron over her plain dress. When she learned that we had no ability to cook that first evening, she returned with a large platter of scrambled eggs and toast slathered with butter.

With the intellect of her youngest child, she had married a rough guy who earned his living by hauling stuff in his truck. Mr. Epstein was loud and crude. However, he treated his simple wife with a joking kind of affection. Didn't he notice that her skin was rough, her facial expression a bit blank, her appearance dowdy, and her sentences basic?

For my part, I was happy enough to run and bike with Irwin. Saturday nights were taken with watching the *Jackie Gleason Show* at the Epstein's home. We would first walk to the candy store to purchase long pretzel sticks and chocolate ice cream for the entire family with Mr. Epstein's money. Then, we would settle on the living room floor to watch. Mr. Epstein occupied the stuffed recliner. Mrs. Epstein pulled in a chair from the kitchen. Despite their obvious lack of money, they never begrudged my presence.

Suddenly, it struck me. Mr. Epstein was playing Gleason's Ralph Kramden to Emily, who he saw as Audrey Meadow's Alice Kramden. They were living as The Honeymooners, only Emily Epstein was unaware that she was acting a role.

"Can I get you some coffee?" Mrs. Epstein might ask.

"Honey, you're the greatest," Mr. Epstein would reply.

Their mutt, the one Emily took in because it had been wandering the streets bedraggled and abandoned, was fed fried eggs covered in powdered sugar – just like what she fed her children. Her province was cooking and keeping the house clean. She sent her children to shop for groceries because handling money was too confusing. Mr. Epstein made up the grocery list and every other decision for the family.

"Look baby, I'm going out to buy a new car. What color do you like?"

"I like purple."

Sure enough, Mr. Epstein returned with a two-tone, purple and white Dodge DeSoto. When he took us for a maiden ride, we knew to keep the passenger window rolled up on the driver's side to avoid cigar smoke and periodic spittle that he released out the window.

"Oh, what a lovely car," she remarked. "And, I like it that you blow your smoke and spit out the window."

"You're a riot, Emily," Mr. Epstein gently retorted knowing that her comment held no subtle criticism.

As soon as we returned from showing the car off, Emily prepared a snack for Mr. Epstein.

"That was hard, buying a new car. Scrambled or fried?"

Blissful ignorance is a comfort, I suppose. No arguing, no depressing thoughts about whether life is offering what we imagine we want, no startling highs or great disappointments. What is offered is accepted. Mrs. Epstein never complained.

For his part, Mr. Epstein showed kindness and consideration to his child-wife. At worst, he would sometimes joke when Emily did something particularly dimwitted.

"To the moon, Emily, to the moon!"

I often marveled how differently the Epstein's interacted from the way our family argued, disputed, cajoled, and strove to get ahead. The Epstein's behaved without rancor toward each other.

Perhaps, Mr. Epstein realized his limitations. By marrying someone who demanded nothing, he would never be challenged at home or doubt his competence. She made him feel important. In return, he treated her grandly. That was their bargain.

I lost track of the family after we moved. My fantasy was that the youngest, Herman, would become a physician. He would refuse to settle for a life of scrambled or fried eggs.

Life

Mary Anne likes clipping food advertisements because "for a little effort why not save a few cents?" My approach favors supermarkets that maintain lower prices and higher quality across the board, so I don't have to sweat the small stuff. No right or wrong, no arguments, no shopping together, and no criticism. Cue the happy bird music.

"Marv, I want some Life cereal. Take this coupon, please. It is good at the Giant supermarket chain."

While I would ordinarily invoke our agreement, my spouse was under the weather. And, we know from experience when something matters to our partner. On this morning, Life cereal mattered.

"Sure. I'll be back in a jiffy."

"Don't forget the skim milk," she yelled as I closed the front door.

Nothing is more confusing to me than lots of noise and colors and flashing signs and people moving. That is why I generally avoid malls around the holidays. That is why I would probably do better with blinders when confusion reigns. That is why I carefully studied the variously sized boxes of Life cereal, some with cinnamon and some original, at our crowded Giant supermarket. It was Christmas time; the store was replete with specials and people and color and noise.

I noticed that the store brand's checkered squares were priced lower than the Life coupon special.

Sticking with the request (another lesson learned the hard way), I placed two boxes of regular sized Life cereal – one cinnamon and one original – into my cart. I quickly rolled to the check-out counter to avoid any more distractions.

"Oh, I have a coupon."

"I'm sorry sir, these coupons are valid only for specially sized boxes."

I really, really hate it when I am behind someone who causes a delay in the supermarket check-out line. Didn't you notice your item was not marked with the fifty percent discount? Didn't you see that the applesauce jar had a crack? Why isn't your credit card valid? On this day, I was the guy who was causing the wait while my issue was resolved, while other lines sped merrily along, and while other customers silently fumed.

"Call a manager. I came here specifically to use the coupon."

The young supervisor pulled me aside while everyone watched.

"We don't have the item in stock," he smiled. "It did not come in with our last shipment."

"Well, I think you should discount my purchase."

"Let me explain how it works," he patiently told me. "Think of coupons as a game. Sometimes you win; sometimes the store wins."

"And . . .?"

"You did not win today."

He was right. I had unexpectedly bumped against bureaucracy and rigidness. Saving his company a few cents on a box or two of Life was more important to this supervisor than my getting a bargain. But, I could still win the game of life with Mary Anne.

"Honey, I got two different boxes of Life cereal," I immediately yelled upon walking into the kitchen.

"Great, where's the skim milk?"

That Old Gang of Mine

After my rich high school friends and I drove to the Peter Pan diner for a late-night snack, we got into a playful food fight. We flung whipped cream onto mirrors, tossed and smeared blueberry pie filling onto seats, and spilled drinks onto the table and floor. We paid and left laughing.

I didn't fling the whipped cream, toss around the blueberry filling, or purposefully throw drinks. But, I was participating as an enabler. I had not objected. Just as an audience is important to performers, my presence acquiesced in their antics.

What about the waitress who cleaned up? What about the owner who absorbed the cost for broken dishware? What about the other customers who hurriedly left? I was ashamed, then and now.

The final straw happened when we returned to Jersey by public bus after seeing a rock show in New York City. On the way back, my good friends started clowning around by hanging off straps and making rude noises. An elderly lady voiced her complaint from her seat without looking at us – "They act like hoodlums!" I told her we were not hurting anyone, only fooling around. She refused to acknowledge my words.

I had not swung on the bus handles or made obnoxious sounds. I had not offended the other passengers or made the bus driver's ride miserable. But, I had not objected to their behavior. After that incident, I left the group. It took over a year to make new friends.

That brings me to people who don't object when our political rights are insulted, when folks with whom we don't readily relate are abused, or when injustice occurs elsewhere.

We are the enablers who defend, justify, rationalize, and explain, even in our silence. We leave it to others to clean up the whipped cream.

Wants and Needs

Are holiday celebrations an attempt to ward of winter's gloom by carving turkey, lighting candles, decorating pine trees, and drinking? As social beings, do we gather against the darkness like herd animals? Do we ply each other with gifts as a form of grooming?

Felix Adler (founder of Ethical Culture) conjectured that human beings have an existential (fundamental) fear of isolation. Because we are alone in ourselves and in the great universe, we seek solace through relationships that afford an opportunity to bring meaning to our lives through contact. We desperately hold onto those with whom we have some affection even when they are no longer with us.

When my older sister took her life, I was devastated. When I arrived at her too lonely apartment, Dad and Helen Levinson – a family friend – were sorting through her pitiful belongings.

"Take the television, Marvin. She would have wanted you to have it."

I know Helen's words were meant as solace. Yet, they felt like an icicle stabbing my pain. What right had Helen to inform me about what Mary might want? Why would I need a television to remind me that my sister was dead?

Let's donate these items to charity," I suggested. "Let's take one item of remembrance for each family member."

I took a piece of pottery – a handcrafted vase - in which Mary had placed a branch sprayed with white paint. It was a token that represented her love of things beautiful before the darkness took possession.

Perhaps, the rationale for gatherings, for caring, and for kindness are less important than the need.

About The Author

Marv Friedlander lives in Fairfax, Virginia, with his wife, Mary Anne. They have two children, Sarah and Joseph, who put up with Friedlander's offbeat sense of humor. He also has two children from a former marriage: Peter, who lives in Maryland, and Hal, who lives in Brooklyn. He has worked at the IRS and at a pizza joint, learning as much from making pizza as from auditing the tax returns of nonprofit organizations. There is room everywhere for tolerance, respect, and kindness.

Marv Friedlander

Friedlander is the author of *Felix Speaks: Adler's Ethical Culture*, which offers a fun and insightful examination of the philosophy and life of noted humanist and social reformer Felix Adler. He also wrote *Du Bois Speaks*, a book detailing W. E. B. Du Bois's efforts to promote human rights.

Made in the USA
Lexington, KY
23 January 2018